"Rebecca Caigoy ... a spiritual adventure story with such a fast-moving plot that I found impossible to put the book down after I started to read it. It is also a spiritual guidebook, filled with wisdom about trusting God in difficult times. An additional attractive feature of the book is its combination of practical application and quoted passages from the Bible."

Leland Ryken, Ph.D.
Author of *How to Read the Bible as Literature*,
Words of Delight: A Literary Introduction to the Bible,
and 43 other books
Professor, Wheaton College and Global University

"Rebecca's story is one of radical trust in God despite the enemy's numerous efforts to destroy her life. I was riveted by her experiences and didn't want to put the book down. My faith was strengthened as I read about how God miraculously intervened over and over in her life. The prayers and reflective questions at the end made each chapter personal, as I examined my own heart and how I have responded during hardships. Rebecca has a humble and gentle spirit about her, yet also an inner strength and boldness that have enabled her to persevere. I highly recommend this book to anyone who has ever wondered if God cares, if He sees, if He knows.... Her book is a firm reminder that He will never leave us or forsake us."

Jaimie Bowman
Minister, Speaker, and
Author of *Breathe: 31 Moments with God {for Moms}*

"Rebecca's story is one of perseverance, faith, and prayer."
Barbara Gilliam, D. Min
President, Women in Ministry, SoCal Network AG
Former Pastor of Glad Tidings Assembly

"Rebecca's beautiful book came to me at a very difficult time in my life. Her words were a true inspiration. I was impressed how she correlated stories in the Bible with situations she herself had gone through. Rebecca's honesty and willingness to share the most difficult times in her life was incredible. Her faith and total trust in the Lord Jesus Christ, as she walked through life and death situations, will certainly inspire the readers of this wonderful book."

Joyce Moss
Uganda Outreach Coordinator, Free Lance Ministries
Former Coordinator for Asia, Aglow International

"How exciting to see a lifelong dream comes to pass! And then for that fulfilled dream to be a story of God's guidance and faithfulness in the life of one who desires to follow Him with all her heart! May God use it to lead many people into a desire for and experience of a deeper intimacy with Him."

Jim Gutel
Dean, SoCal School of Ministry

I have known Rev. Rebecca Caigoy and her ministry for about ten years. She has a heart for the lost and a keen interest in discipling new believers. Her book is a beautiful production based on her passion and the inspiration of the Spirit. I wish her and the readers well as this work will be a great inspiration.

George Pallil, Ph.D.
Professor, Latin American Bible College
Pastor, South Pasadena Assembly
Presbyter, LA Section, SoCal Network

LIVING LIFE
in the
Shadow of Death

by
Rebecca Ducil-Caigoy

Copyright © 2015 by Rebecca Ducil-Caigoy

LIVING LIFE in the Shadow of Death
by Rebecca Ducil-Caigoy

Printed in the United States of America.

ISBN 9781498432214

All rights reserved solely by the author. The author guarantees all contents are original and do not infringe upon the legal rights of any other person or work. No part of this book may be reproduced in any form without the permission of the author. The views expressed in this book are not necessarily those of the publisher.

Unless otherwise indicated, Scripture quotations taken from the Holy Bible, New International Version, Copyright @ 1973, 1978, 1984 by International Bible Society. Used by permission of Zondervan Publishing House. All rights reserved. The NIV Minister's Bible. Hendrickson Publishers, LLC.

Scripture quotations taken from the New American Standard Bible (NASB). Copyright © 1960, 1962, 1963, 1968, 1971, 1972, 1973, 1975, 1977, 1995 by The Lockman Foundation. Used by permission. All rights reserved.

Scripture quotations taken from the New Living Translation (NLT). Copyright © 1996, 2004, 2007 by Tyndale House Foundation. Used by permission. All rights reserved.

Scripture quotations taken from the English Standard Version (ESV). Copyright © 2001 by Crossway, a publishing ministry of Good News Publishers. Used by permission. All rights reserved.

Scripture quotations taken from the New King James Version (NKJV). Copyright © 1979, 1980, 1982 by Thomas Nelson, Inc. Used by permission. All rights reserved.

Scripture quotations taken from the King James Version (KJV) – public domain

www.xulonpress.com

This book is dedicated
to
My beloved children: Revena, Leandro, and Levi
who are my precious jewels I daily wear with
prayers for God's best for their lives.

My ever loving, supportive, and faithful
husband Leo,
who has been my critic and encourager

My father, Fermin M. Ducil
who inspired and motivated me when I was young
to dream for the future and chase it to fruition.

My Heavenly Father
who breathed life into my being
and gave me gifts to fulfill His purpose.

TABLE OF CONTENTS

Dedication.................................v
Introduction..............................ix

Part I: The Emerging – Where Am I Going?
Chapter 1 – The First Emergency.............19
Chapter 2 – Month of Ordeal.................25
Chapter 3 – Trip Abroad.....................31
Chapter 4 – The Year in Retrospect..........44

Part II: The Sudden – This Is It!
Chapter 5 – New Year, Here I Come...........55
Chapter 6 – The Fatal Blow..................63

Part III: The Aftermath – What Now, My Lord?
Then..80
Chapter 7 – Stand Firm......................86
Chapter 8 – Be Still........................97
Chapter 9 – Move On........................103

Part IV: The Recollections – Dangers and Toils!
Chapter 10 – Escape from Fire..............115
Chapter 11 – Threats on Waters.............131
Chapter 12 – Battle in the Womb............152

Part V: The Restoration
Chapter 13 – Rest to Refresh 162
Chapter 14 – Rebound to Abound. 176
Chapter 15 – Extend to Expand 190

Afterword 211
Bonus Article – Travails and Triumphs of an
Evangelist 221
Acknowledgments. 227
Bible Translations 235
Notes. 237
Letter and Prayer for the Reader. 245
About the Author. 249

INTRODUCTION

I was about eight years old when my father interrupted my childhood chores with a question, "What do you like to be when you grow up?"

Enmeshed with religiosity and in an innocent quirk, I replied, "I'd like to become a nun."

"Oh!" My father's countenance changed from anticipation to sullenness. His jaw dropped. Then, he uttered words of anxiety for my future founded on the world's standard of success and prosperity.

Years passed. I was already in high school when my father, tenacious and resolute, approached me again with the same question. That time, my answer was gently emphatic. My one sentence rebuttal did not modify his dream for me. I picked up a book, showed him the title page, and said, "Someday, you will see my name here."

I often heard him interjecting the advantage of being a lady lawyer. Obviously, he was indirectly telling me to take up law after graduation from high school the following year. On all those occasions, I succeeded in maintaining my silence. His illustrations and convincing words didn't break my silence into compliance.

Many things happened in the germination and development since the seed was planted. The hand of the Maker, Planter, and Potter was in full control.

Soon after graduation from high school, I was writing poetry. Writing remained my heartthrob throughout college. Out of the 20 poems written in college days, three were published. I also ventured into writing short stories. One unpublished commercially, another in the university magazine.

I realized my potential when I discovered I could write in a time-pressured qualifying exam. I passed the test to join the staff of the university paper with newspaper and magazine publications. It opened the door for me to also write news articles as a News Reporter, to create sketches accompanying the contributions, and even designed the cover for a summer issue of the magazine.

Introduction

However, I succumbed to the wishes of my father by enrolling in a pre-law course. My tug of war was strongly bent towards avoiding disappointing my beloved father. He was contented and delighted by my obedience, but he couldn't suppress my innate passion for creative writing.

After stepping out the walls of the university, marriage, motherhood, and career have occupied my time and energy. Years have gone by like precious diamonds that slipped from my hands unnoticed. Until one evening, I met the God of the Bible, living, breathing, and speaking through His Word. Aside from the many discoveries about life and myself, one thing that happened was the resurgence of my love for writing. I wrote a sequel to my poem "Lament," titled it "Lament No More," and dubbed the two "Twin Poems" in a side-by-side presentation.

Fast forward. The opportunity and privilege to serve as a staff in a church office came. In that office, I prayed for God to use me with the gifts He gave. One of His answers was my preparing the Sunday bulletin. I enjoyed every bit of the job. Other writing opportunities followed such as initiating a newsletter for a local Women's Aglow Fellowship, news articles for Christian events, and contributing art reviews on art exhibits of Christian artists for a local newspaper. Although I was not compensated for these writings outside my church job, the sense of accomplishment and fulfillment in actualizing my gift is beyond monetary gains.

Remarkable changes and challenges along life's journey limited my writing activities to papers about my biblical studies interspersed with my continuing education in the graduate school. My desire for creative writing, fiction or non-fiction, remained a longing. The force of circumstances surpassed my longing.

After years of stagnation, at last, creative writing was resurrected. By the second half of 2010, I started to write again. This is something I love to do and not just to dabble in. I decided to write a book. At first, I was grappling for words like someone groping in the dark. It seemed I had forgotten how to write. The words "but live and will proclaim what the Lord has done" in Psalm 118:17 (NIV) were like waterfalls that kept cascading down my mind. With peace and confidence from above, I began writing. The endeavor encountered delays and danger of impossibility. After writing four chapters, my manuscript was accidentally deleted from my computer file. Frustrated and discouraged, I stopped writing.

Faced with financial needs, my days thereafter were absorbed in job search and short courses (free or minimal fee) to qualify for a job. After two years I began to work. The downside of it all was my book writing attempt became at risk for total oblivion and death. Then, the job was short lived and "...all things work together for good..." (Romans 8:28a KJV). On bended knees and open heart, I prayed for God to help me recall what I had written. He did grant the desires of my heart and has carried me through all the way to the last chapter. His divine connections provided encouragement and inspiration from a writing conference, authors, writers, a writing class, and His favor through Xulon Publishing. All these are beyond my wildest imagination, more than I ever thought possible in my younger years when I had revealed my dream to my father – but I did not have an inkling how it would happen.

Despite the delays, risks, and hopelessness, God's story must be written. I must proclaim His life in my temporary, ephemeral, fragile body. I am here today, but will be gone any time. The story you will read is a demonstration of His omnipotent work of His perfect, sovereign will in my borrowed life. Undoubtedly, the gift of writing was saved from extinction that His purpose might be fulfilled. Whatever gift we receive from Him should be used to make known the Giver and His works so He will be glorified. God's gifts are to enable us to partner with Him to fulfill His Word in our lives on earth as it is in heaven.

"For the earth shall be filled with the knowledge of the glory of the Lord as the waters cover the sea." (Habakkuk 2:14 KJV)

God has a story in each of our lives. This is not my story. This is His story written in the timeline of His life in me. I'm just His scribe translating into words His bountiful outpouring of enormous and extravagant love displayed with phenomenal protection, intervention, and deliverance. My life is His life. My story is His story.

Approximately fifty-four years have passed since that father-daughter conversation. The will of my Heavenly Father prevailed.

It is my prayer that you, too, will be blessed and touched by His loving powerful Presence as you read this book. May you be captivated by His voice

Introduction

as you read His Word along with the story. May you hear Him speak to build your faith in Him and Him alone – to be strengthened in your inner being so you will be encouraged to live for Him and others.

Come. Please join me in this promenade of God's marvelous works while living His life. Be blessed, my friend.

PART I

THE EMERGING – WHERE AM I GOING?

CHAPTER 1
THE FIRST EMERGENCY

"My flesh and my heart may fail,
But God is the strength of my heart
and my portion forever." NASB
Psalm 73:26

"When my skin sags and my bones get brittle,
God is rock-firm and faithful" MSG
Psalm 73:26

June 28, 2009 was the first time I ever experienced being in an emergency room of a hospital. I had no option but to go there that late evening. I wasn't really tired that day, tired in the sense that I had to exert much energy to get things done. Why did my blood pressure go up so high when I maintained a healthy diet and exercise? Oh yes, I always took my Atenolol[1] too.

Should I just drink more water? Should I just condition my mind to rest and fight the fear that was engulfing my whole being? Maybe if I just lie down, rest and sleep, my blood pressure will go down and eventually be normal again. But why is my blood pressure still high? I am getting scared. If I don't go to the hospital, something might happen to me while in bed. I can't sleep. I am afraid to sleep. My blood pressure may continue to rise while I'm asleep and a stroke could happen. I must do something to prevent any possibility of stroke. How?

I was having headaches already. I was feeling something different in my body. I didn't like the strange feeling, the numbness, and the pain. It wasn't a striking pain – just a mild sort of. There was slight chest pain and my hands were beginning to shake and arms to numb. It was almost midnight. I decided to call two of my friends who have a doctor friend. I thank God for friends who are willing to help even when inconvenienced at a very "unholy" hour. Incidentally, their doctor friend was on night duty at the hospital. I was able to contact him and was readily accommodated. I was instructed to see him

The First Emergency

immediately. My husband and I rushed to go to the hospital where he was. However, I needed a thorough examination as soon as possible. So, I was referred to another hospital.

There, I was attended to soon because of my emergency situation. After going through the process and waiting, I was told to go inside the emergency room. For the first time in my whole life, I would lie down in an emergency bed. Reality was getting real. This was it. I didn't like what was going on, but I had to be strong, face reality, and obey the nurse's orders. My husband was not allowed to be beside me anymore. I was feeling alone, but not actually alone, because the medical staff was around. My God was with me. I kept on praying, conversing with my living God intermittently from the time I sensed something wrong was happening in my body. Tests, doctor's queries, monitoring equipment, and dextrose pervaded the scenario. All the while, I prayed softly. "Lord, please take charge, let the tests be just confirmations that you are taking care of me, that I'm fine and there's nothing serious to contend with."

I needed to be quiet and contain my questions in my thoughts. I didn't want to stay longer. But if it was necessary and would do me good, I had to be still, wait patiently, and trust God. "Thank you Lord!" I exclaimed deep within. He truly gives peace. The doctor came back and uttered the good news I was hoping to hear.

"You will be released by 6:00 p.m."

Barely a month and a half after, I was in the emergency room again in the same hospital. This time, I stayed longer, slept a night, and was released the following day.

The First Emergency

Let's Pray Together

*"I also tell you this:
If two of you agree down here on earth concerning
anything you ask, my Father in heaven
will do it for you."* NLT
Matthew 18:19

Gracious Lord,

Here I am, not knowing what will come my way today. Nevertheless, I thank You God for knowing everything that concerns me. I thank You that You are in my life. You know that for anything that happens for the first time in my life, I will be anxious and scared. Thank You that You are in control of them all. Thank You for providing a way when I need help. Please bless the divine connections You give, whether their help is out of duty or out of concern. You are their reward. Thank You for being reachable and available whenever I call for help. How soon You respond to my SOS. You're always there whenever I call Your name, Your mighty name, Jesus, Amen.

Reflective Questions

1. Have you experienced being in an emergency room in the hospital?

   _____

   _____

2. How did you deal with health issues in your life?

   _____

   _____

   _____

3. Have you shared about your health with other people or were you willing to share them with others? If not, why?

   _____

   _____

   _____

4. How did changes in your health affect your faith in God and your relationship with Him?

   _____

   _____

CHAPTER 2
MONTH OF ORDEAL

*"Wait on the Lord; Be of good courage,
And He shall strengthen your heart;
Wait, I say, on the Lord!"* NKJV
Psalm 27:14

*"I wait for the Lord, my soul waits,
And in His word do I hope."* NKJV
Psalm 130:5

The following month, I was in the urgent care of a health center. It was a follow up to my first emergency. The ordeal I went through this time was a twice a week repeated checkups and follow ups for three consecutive weeks. The uneasiness of being unproductive made me feel useless. These past months, my activities had been hampered due to those seemingly unending health concerns. They had stripped off my precious time. Were they wasted times? Yes and no.

Yes, because my target schedules had to be rearranged. Some activities had to halt. Each visit consumed almost a day that zapped my zest to be active the remaining few hours of the day. The long hours of waiting at the health center made me more desperate for God's intervention and manifest presence. I needed Him to maintain my composure – to be still, to be quiet, trusting in Him.

No, because this is necessary for health issues to be resolved. Hopefully, soon, this would be over. Nevertheless, I managed to make use of my waiting time by reading my textbooks for my graduate study. Yes, my mind would be occupied with spiritual and intellectual stuff. My mind wouldn't have any room for fear, doubt, or anxiety. Not a bit of those negatives. Sometimes, I would pray softly trying to maintain my spiritual connection, not because of religiosity but because of inner trust of an omnipresent, omnipotent God, yet relational and reliable in His promises. I was reminded of scripture songs. I hummed them softly with the lyrics and melody running through my mind like a CD played on a stereo.

The faith within slowly soared up higher. I was getting stronger... stronger to fight the humdrum of waiting and the routines week after week... stronger to fight the attacks on my faith... stronger to fight the engulfing anxiety which could snuff out a hopeful bright tomorrow.

The first week of September, 2009 passed. Hopefully, this time I would be alright. But after a few days of observation I had to go back to the health center. Oh! How I wished I wouldn't go back there again. Two weeks in a row was enough. I was wrong. My hope remained a hope, just a seemingly futile hope. The prescriptions didn't work well with my body. It was already the third week of the month. My hope was waning. I had to fight within to be sustained and hold on to whatever meager ounce of hope remained. I had to go back again to the health center. There was nothing I could do but to tell the doctor that my body was reacting to the medicine Norvas[1]. The prescription didn't do any better for my blood pressure. There I had to undergo the same process and the time-consuming waiting. In that scenario where I was among many waiting for their number or name to be called, I needed to exercise patience and endurance. After many hours of waiting, my name was called for the nurse to check my vital signs. Then I had to wait again and that next round of waiting was not for a little while. I calmed myself with the thought that the next step of waiting was already for a doctor to examine me. I should welcome each unpleasant atmosphere to win the test for grace and gentleness under pressure. While some showed signs of restlessness or boredom, I should make a difference.

Most often, I would be there in the morning and then leave in the afternoon, sometimes late afternoon. Yes, it was a long process, but it was worth the waiting, complete with a new prescription that worked well with my body.

Those weeks were becoming a torture to me. To top it all, I was scheduled to leave for a trip out of the country. The torture that was becoming to be didn't come. I didn't allow it. I was looking forward to my planned trip.

Let's Pray Together

*"I also tell you this:
If two of you agree down here on earth concerning
anything you ask, my Father in heaven
will do it for you."* NLT
Matthew 18:19

Gracious Lord,
Thank You for Your sovereign power to sustain me in seemingly unending tests of faith. You strengthen me inside to overcome what is happening in the outside. You help me bear the length of days of waiting and hoping. How can I grumble, how can I complain? You are the faithful God at all times, the ever present help in times of need, in times of trouble. Please forgive me when I'm tempted to feel uneasy; but let my eyes be fixed on You. Please take charge that I may not be overtaken by the discomforting, destabilizing situation of my present cares. Let me stand on the solid ground of Your truth because You are the eternally permanent God who has the sole authority over my temporal needs. Truly, there is an end to anything temporary and You make Your peace in me permanent. Thank You, Father God, in Jesus' name, Amen.

Reflective Questions

1. Have you experienced waiting for results of any kind? What was it and how did it feel in the process?

   _____

   _____

   _____

2. How did you overcome the drudgery and monotony of waiting?

   _____

   _____

   _____

3. Why is waiting a test of faith?

   _____

   _____

   _____

4. What is your comment on the phrase "wait on the Lord?"

   _____

   _____

   _____

CHAPTER 3
TRIP ABROAD

"For this reason we also, since the day we heard it, do not cease to pray for you, and to ask that you may be filled with the knowledge of His will in all wisdom and spiritual understanding; that you may walk worthy of the Lord, fully pleasing Him being fruitful in every good work and increasing in the knowledge of God." NKJV
Colossians 1:9-10

Should I go to the Philippines or should I not? This Hamlet-like[1] question put me into a deadlock. After going through all the health concerns the prior month, should I proceed with my trip? Didn't I need a respite from any activity with a trip overseas? My pragmatic husband wanted me to cancel the flight. Would costs for cancellation of my flight validate my preference to go ahead? On the other hand, was my choice a bolstering faith beyond lack of wisdom? My husband once said to me, "but faith does not discount wisdom."

Finally, the determining factor for the decision was that the last prescription restored my body's condition before my scheduled flight. This fact coupled with fervent prayers & faith in the full control of my omnipotent, omnipresent God prevailed in my decision to go. Whenever, wherever, however He wants me to go home to Him, it will happen – and I don't have any control over His perfect will. Let His perfect will rule. His time is the perfect time for me to depart this sin-laden, chaotic world.

Arriving on the other side of the earth showed contrasts of the life I lived in the last six years (2003-2009) here in the U.S. from the prior years before I came here: the tropical country of the Philippines, the Filipino people, the climate – humid. I was excited to see my first son again and his daughter, who is my second granddaughter, for the first time. She was almost a year old. It was worth all the preparations for the trip and the time, expenses, and effort for several months - just to purchase and accumulate the stuff and goodies, including those for my granddaughter's first birthday and dedication. All these strivings were despite my financial struggles.

The excitement and happiness were shortened. The scene soon changed into trauma. Unpleasant incidents happened. Furthermore, the climate in the Philippines is hot and humid. My body clock had to adjust. It fairly did. With the changes, new faces, and sour incidents, I felt like a stranger in my own house where my whole family once resided. Also, what I hoped wouldn't happen, did happen. My blood pressure shot up again. My prescriptions seemed to lose their effectiveness. Days and nights became struggles warring for life. I fought the thought of going to a hospital. In the Philippines, a patient can't receive medical attention without a deposit. My finances were only enough for my travel. Nothing was left except my dependence on God's word in Jeremiah 33:3,

"Call to me, and I will answer you, and show you great and mighty things, which you do not know." (NKJV)

I remember this was the same verse my husband and I prayed with when our youngest son, Levi, who was barely a few weeks old, was near-death. In the middle of the night, he was suffocated. His nose was clogged with milk I was breastfeeding him. My eyes were so heavy, body tired from household chores and still regaining strength from childbirth, I slept unknowingly. All of a sudden, I woke up and saw his eyes closed. He seemed like just sleeping, but his whole body was bluish – stiff – not moving. Alarmed, I called my husband. We tried to wake him up, but no sound came out. We laid hands on him and prayed with God's challenge and promise in Jeremiah 33:3. We persevered in prayer for more minutes, holding on to His promise. Then, He did show us His great work we had never experienced ever. The baby cried; slowly . . . his eyes opened, then . . . his body moved. Our voices burst into unstoppable praises, instantly and spontaneously. We rejoiced with worship songs as my husband was cuddling and swaying our baby Levi.

The sight of the house I once held dear alienated me. I held the house dear, not for the material things, but the feeling of home. It was the place my family gathered together and family is precious to me. As a young girl, I didn't have lofty ambitions. All I dreamed of was to have a happy home in a house of our own. The dream came true. In fact, it was already our second house. Sitting alone and scanning around contemplatively, my mind was coming to grip with reality (like tangible things beside me, I can easily touch them one by one) such as: the loss of things a woman would love to acquire for her family (many were missing or destroyed), the absence of two of my three children who would not be back to reside in that home due to their decisions to find their fortunes abroad, the deteriorating house, the emptiness of the room my mother once occupied (she lived with us when she was getting old) – only some of her personal belongings remain. Also, the memory of my mother's battle for life at the hospital till her death added thorn and angst to the thoughts in succession. All these can't be confined to the deep recesses of my mind. I sobbed. Moreover, physical distance with my mother has ended. I thought I had no more tears to cry. But now, tears are useless. I can't resuscitate her. We can't be together anymore.

I became aware of the reality of losses. Isn't it part of change – loss? Yes, it is and I'd better face it bravely. What will I gain with all the losses? Maybe, I'll reread the book, "Gaining Through Losing"[2] authored by Evelyn Christenson.

Despite these grim realities, I regained my composure with scriptures.

"Thank God no matter what happens. This is the way God wants you who belong to Christ Jesus to live" I Thessalonians 5:18 (MSG).

Not that I'm giving thanks for the losses that robbed the joy, but it is God's will for me to give thanks to Him to maintain a grateful attitude in whatever state I am. I should maintain contentment because

"Heaven and earth will pass away, but His Word remains forever" Matthew 24:35 (ESV).

Things and people I have lost are temporary on earth. They cannot be held as long as I want. Only His steadfast love and mercy remain always.

During the nights I was alone in the house, His Presence was overwhelmingly undeniable. Prayers in spiritual battle, in tongues and known tongues, filled the whole house in the middle of those late nights. I fought for my life in the midst of rising blood pressure. God gave this life to me. No one can take it away from me without His consent.

"He who is in me is greater than He who is in the world" 1 John 4:4 (ESV).

The enemy of our soul who is in the world is the author of sickness, chaos, and death.

"The thief comes only to steal and kill and destroy. I came that they may have life and have it abundantly," Jesus' statement in John 10:10 (ESV).

The Holy Spirit armored me to quench the fiery darts of the enemy. He gave me courage and strength to face the war against the death-engulfing spirit in the name of Jesus Christ with the covering of His precious blood by faith. The battle is already won at the cross. As Jesus said, "It is finished" John 19:30 KJV. That was the opportune time to believe, to claim, to speak out – and then win the victory. The battle is won! Victory is mine.

The horrendous nights and days were over. I was ready to speak in a Sunday Service. Again, this showed another season of change. Friends and people I had been involved with in ministries were gone. Sad to say, only a few remained in my former home church. I was speaking to a different crowd. Nevertheless, that fact is less important compared to God's message birthed within me for them. What matters most is to deliver His Word.

Reconnections with fellow ministers in Metro Cebu led to continued speaking commitments, then and in the near future. What joy explodes when you allow yourself to become a vessel of His spoken Word! My spirit danced with joy. As the famous Mark Twain said "On with the dance, let joy be unconfined..."[3]

The day came when one purpose of my travel was fulfilled – to attend my granddaughter's dedication and first birthday. To witness the events was a cherished moment. Yet, I resolved to overcome my mixed emotions, to win over the feelings of regret that I was there, and overcome the pain within.

"I can do all things through Christ who strengthens me," Philippians 4:13 (NKJV).

Faking smiles? No. The positive has triumphed over the negative. I must be true to what I taught the children in my five years of children ministry. The melody of the song "With Christ in my Vessel"[4] resounded in my heart and mind, reminding me of the inner joy that caused a genuine smile on my face during the baby dedication service and at the birthday celebration.

Those special events ended. My next itinerary was to visit my mother's graveside. On the way to the cemetery, the gnawing anguish resurfaced. So, I held any teardrop from falling. I wrestled myself from crying, until I reached the tomb. I sighed, "This is it."

In a few instances during our telephone conversation overseas, I had told her, "Please wait a little more. I will be back and we will travel together where you want to go." She wanted to visit her hometown in Leyte and her relatives. She's gone. She couldn't wait any longer and off she went. She had to go to her eternal home. I consoled myself with the thought that she's in a better place. She had accepted Jesus Christ as her personal Savior and Lord and had been reading the enlarged Bible I gave her even when I was away from her.

The remaining days swiftly passed. I had to prepare for my return flight. Then, an unsurprising call with unexpected message came from my niece Melody. Her brother who had been sick for a long time finally passed away. She was requesting my immediate presence and help because her parents were coming from the United States. So, after an inter-island trip to my mother's relatives, I needed to travel again – this time to Metro Manila, the capital region in the north, a far place from the middle region where I previously resided in that country.

"Oh God, please make me strong to comfort my bereaved relatives," I prayed. I was thankful for Susan, a church friend who helped me procure a flight at a rush hour. Someway, somehow, the happiness of relatives seeing each other after many years alleviated the pain of another loss in the family. Moreover, it was God's opportune time for me to be useful for Him anywhere I would be. I conducted the funeral service in the cemetery and many heard the truth about life and death.

I came back to Cebu and resumed my preparation for my flight back to the U.S. My scheduled flight was postponed due to this fortuitous event.

As the scripture says in Romans 8:28 NKJV,

". . . all things work together for good to those who love God, to those who are the called according to His purpose."

I had the time to my meet my former church friends, to speak in another church, and attend the funeral of a friend. In the midst of my preparation for my return flight, my church friend, Bing, called informing me about the death of our fellow Aglow leader. Aglow[5] is an international organization originally for women.

"What is this?" I exclaimed.

My high blood pressure, the visit to mother's tomb, inter-island travel to notify relatives of mother's death, death of another relative, and then death again of a friend in ministry... sorrow after sorrow after sorrow... until the last days of my travel were such a battle.

"How can I taste a bit of respite?" I wondered.

Through all the negative circumstances of my Christian life, I've learned to trust in my Savior Jesus. The melody and lyrics of the song , "Through it All"[6] reminded me I wasn't alone. "Thank you, God."

Let's Pray Together

*"I also tell you this:
If two of you agree down here on earth concerning
anything you ask, my Father in heaven
will do it for you."* NLT
Matthew 18:19

Gracious Lord,
Thank You for the spirit of wisdom at all times especially when I need it most. You have filled me with the knowledge of Your Word, of Your Truth that guides my renewed mind and quickens my mortal body. You are with my plans and You direct my path. I won't be afraid because You will go before me and smoothen the rough road ahead of me. Thank You for taking charge of my journeys in life and for Your provisions for all the travels in the past and in the coming days, months, and years. How marvelous are Your provisions. You also established peace in my heart to thwart away fears of dangers and death along the way and the places I go. You are the way, the truth, and the life; You are my Savior, Redeemer, and friend. Thank You Father God for the strength and comfort You lovingly give when I face different kinds of losses in life. I am contented with Your sufficient peace with what is left. With You, little becomes enough, little becomes more. Thank You for Your abiding Presence wherever I am.

I give You all praises due to Your wonderful name, Jesus, I pray, Amen.

Reflective Questions

1. What kind of losses have you encountered in life?

   _____

   _____

   _____

2. Which of those losses hurt you the most? Why?

   _____

   _____

   _____

3. How did you cope with the bitter reality of a loss?

   _____

   _____

   _____

4. How do you look at the future after the loss/losses?

   _____

   _____

   _____

CHAPTER 4
THE YEAR IN RETROSPECT

"I don't mean to say that I have already achieved these things or that I have already reached perfection! But I keep working toward that day when I will finally be all that Christ Jesus saved me for and wants me to be. No, dear brothers and sisters, I am still not all I should be, but I am focusing all my energies on this one thing: forgetting the past and looking forward to what lies ahead, I strain to reach the end of the race and receive the prize for which God, through Jesus Christ, is calling us up to heaven."
Philippians 3:12-14 (NLT)

How did 2009 start? Almost five years have passed as of this writing. The year began with looming unpredictability. Unsettling changes were becoming obvious.

The Year In Retrospect

One Sunday morning in January, I noticed something unusual. I sensed I was out of place. For clarity and curiosity, I inquired the lead pastor of my home church then. I was informed that my ministry assignment would be to assist a daughter church in their Bible studies in Carson City. With this development and previous arrangements cancelled, I understood why the assignment led to my dismay.

Difficulty in transportation, schedules, and distance were impediments to rendering the services. An array of questions ran through my mind. Public transport in that city is provided only up to 8:00 p.m. Most Bible studies are in the evenings. How could I get a transport from the Bible study venue to the train station? Would the Bible study host give me a ride? Maybe yes, maybe not.

How about my preparation for a new ministry? How can I do it? Will I have the time involving myself in Bible studies in Carson while residing in another city? In this city, I was also asked to teach a Bible study for a Saturday outreach in another church.

Soon, I chose the second option to lessen the stresses that accompany motley changes. I was in the process of adjusting to my new residence; thus, commuting and working in another city would be burdensome. At least my pioneering ministry and the Bible study outreach will be in the same city.

The first quarter of the year can be aptly described as decisive – launching into deeper depths of service, treading an untrodden path, embracing the challenge of the unknown.

Like a pensive soliloquy, I started questioning myself, *who am I, a petite brown woman in her fifties daring to pioneer a ministry outside her country of origin? Are you crazy? Are you overestimating yourself? You're out of wisdom. You're only enthusiastic.*

Should I entertain these thoughts or brush them aside? Should I ignore the rhema[1] in Habakkuk 2:14 and other verses years ago that continue to reverberate with me as years passed by?

> *"For the earth shall be filled with the knowledge of the glory of the Lord as the waters cover the sea."* (KJV)

How about the events equipping me for these tasks for the past 33 years in churches, in ministries, in Bible schools, in conferences, in seminars, and in my personal life? All these have trained and molded me one step at a time. Each step was a sacrificial service, a grateful offering.

What now? Shall I take risks again – risks with unsurprising expectation? Yes, I would. Life is full of uncertainties. The only certain and safest thing about life is to be in the center of God's perfect will. I have chosen the path less travelled (especially for women); and I have the peace and joy because Jesus took control of my life – His Word will never pass away.

". . . in Me you may have peace. In the world you will have tribulation; but be of good cheer, I have overcome the world." John 16:33 (NKJV)

"Blessed are those who are persecuted for righteousness' sake, for theirs is the kingdom of heaven." Matthew 5:10 (NKJV)

"We are hard-pressed on every side, yet not crushed; we are perplexed, but not in despair; persecuted but not forsaken; struck down, but not destroyed." 2 Corinthians 4:8-9 (NKJV)

These words of Jesus Christ and encouragement of Apostle Paul were uplifting and developed my strength to fight the good fight of faith.

"Be brave, have courage." I told myself again. It's better to try and fail than not to try at all. "Fail?" I should not entertain the thought of failure.

"Obedience is far better than sacrifice. Listening to him is much better than offering the fat of rams" 1 Samuel 15:22 (NLT).

Jesus' last words and command to His disciples was to

"Therefore, go and make disciples of all nations... Teach these new disciples to obey all the commands I have given you" Matthew 28:19-20 (NLT).

How? God knows my gifts. He gave them after all. He touched me with passion for Him and compassion for lost souls.

Activities such as: connecting with people; making new contacts; establishing acquaintances; reaching out; finding relatives, old friends, and former classmates within the city and the vicinity had occupied my days, weeks, and months. I haven't minded the time, money, and effort spent. Focus has been my main concern.

A line quoted in class by my Bible teacher before, "Only one life will soon be past,"[2] had touched me and charted the route of my new life in Christ.

Before May ended, I conducted a Mother-Daughter event through the courtesy of my home church then. I was allowed to use a room for the specific event. At last! My pioneering ministry had begun. This evangelistic small gathering was followed with "Nothing's Too Hard for God"[3] video series. Even though they were short-lived, eventually I started two home Bible studies. Indeed, my prayers and efforts attained fruition.

Let's Pray Together

*"I also tell you this:
If two of you agree down here on earth concerning
anything you ask, my Father in heaven
will do it for you."* NLT
Matthew 18:19

Gracious Lord,
Thank You for Your faithfulness that never change, never waver, never falter. Year after year You're still the same. Seasons change, but You don't. As I look back, I can't thank You less. Despite the lack of resources, the disappointing changes, and vague direction Your peace remain intact, unshakable in shackling situations and circumstances. Thank You Father God for helping me actualize Your Word, "I can do all things through Christ which strengtheneth me" (Philippians 4:13 KJV). *With all the uncertainties of each year, I can also say "It is well with my soul,"[4] I have survived. To end each year with a grateful heart will surely do me good and exalt Your name. Please help me keep going Lord Jesus, Amen.*

The Year In Retrospect

Reflective Questions

1. Is looking back to the past year or a year ending helpful? If so, why? In what way?

   _____

   _____

   _____

2. What is the difference between "looking back" and "leaving behind?"

   _____

   _____

   _____

3. How is recollecting the past help you in planning your goals?

   _____

   _____

   _____

4. How do your past and present define your life mission and vision?

   _____

   _____

PART II
THE SUDDEN - THIS IS IT!

ANOTHER YEAR

Dominates the sound of firecrackers now
It's new year's eve we know
Cheerful faces, soundful laughter
"Happy New Year," they hail and cry.

Let the old year fade and dim
Welcome nineteen seventy two
Heralding they for it's a year new
Hopeful creatures pronounce and smile.

But people then and now distort
The essence of New Year
It shouldn't be called as such
For it's just another year.

Concepts, attitudes, and practices
Shall it stay or be altered now
Problems, fears, and conflicts
Shall it diminish or reign this time.

Another year, yes it's another year
For us to hope and ponder on
Let it be new and better now,
And not just old another year.

A poem written January 5, 1972 by Rebecca Ducil

CHAPTER 5
NEW YEAR, HERE I COME

Unlike the past year, I welcomed the New Year 2010 with hope and expectations for better things to come. One thing better was the new residence with bigger space and better neighborhood. I welcomed the New Year with open arms and pronounced, "Here I am ready for what you have to offer in my life." I relegated the past to the background with all its pains and hurts and declared, "This is another chance to taste and 'see the goodness of the Lord in the land of the living'" (Psalm 27:13b KJV/NIV/NASB). I wanted to see the brighter side of life this year. Enough of what I had last year, let this year be a better one. There I was... hoping... expecting... anticipating.

Holidays are tiring days. Inevitably, the "busyness" of the season has filled my calendar and to-do list. The post holidays stress was compounded with the transfer of residence. Nevertheless, I managed to go on a partial fasting with my whole month prayer emphasis. Usually, every January, I commit myself to this spiritual discipline to seek God's direction and to strengthen my spiritual muscle for the rest of the coming days. I wanted to be free from the turmoil of the previous year and just bask in God's presence. I have believed that giving God time and priority allows me to sharpen my hearing ears so that seeking God will be earnest and fruitful.

I desperately hungered to know God's will for the season of my life then. After all I had gone through, I felt like David in Psalm 42:1-2,

> *"As the deer pants for streams of water, so my soul pants for you, Oh God. My soul thirsts for God, for the living God. When can I go and meet with God?"* (NIV)

As if I was in a parched dry land, no plant could survive there. I escaped the kaleidoscope of traumatic experiences. Not anymore, not for now, at least. I would rather catch a glimpse of a bright year. I wanted to rest from the exhaustion of striving, of the memory of certain matters, and circumstances beyond my control. I believed this would be the best thing to do – prayer and fasting, a personal reflective retreat.

Except for the daily routines, I wanted to seclude myself and ponder on the following things:

- Ceasing the tendency to try to understand what I didn't and couldn't understand from last year
- Continuing or stopping the search for a job, fulltime or part time
- Guidance for leading the three Bible study groups
- Anointing to deliver His message
- Interceding for souls
- Direction for open doors
- Wisdom for approach and strategy
- Questions about home church, to stay or not to stay.

I was in a state of not knowing what to do. I was helpless without God… I couldn't go on… How could I move forward?

Let the year 2010 be a new beginning, with hopes eventually surging up into fruition. This would be a new year and not just another year of repetitive struggles, strivings, and sadness. Let the year be a year of promise, of pursuit, and of purpose. I wanted to claim God's promises, chase God's pursuits, and catch God's purposes for my life. I longed to advance, achieve, and fulfill what He had planned for me and in store for me that year. I desired to take even just a quick peep of the near future like the prayer song "Just a Little Touch"[1] that expresses hope in Jesus' touch as the source of light that dispels darkness and alleviate the burden of trials and hopelessness. I didn't yearn or wish for a telescopic view... just a clearer vision... perspective... or vantage point.

What steps would I take now? At least I won't be groping in the dark. How I wished for signs or confirmations.

I stopped bargaining with God for these desires. They seem rational and selfless, but my situation should not be the focus. I must seek Him, the knowledge of Him more than before, His character, or to hear from Him and nothing else. An additional agenda will pollute the purity of purpose for such a retreat. It would likewise disqualify even an urgent need such as mine. I should search Him with all of my heart, not a portion of it, or with conditions or demands. I should seek Him looking down on my situation, but totally turned upward with both ears in tune to hear Him say, *"Be still and know that I am God,"* Psalm 46:10 KJV.

Let's Pray Together

*"I also tell you this:
If two of you agree down here on earth concerning
anything you ask, my Father in heaven
will do it for you."* NLT
Matthew 18:19

Gracious Lord,
Thank You for being my hope in life. The uncertainties of the coming days will dissipate because You are the author of time and space. You have the power over all the events among all people in history at all times in all places. I may plan but I don't know what the days, months, and years will bring forth. Father God, I seek You, I search for You. You are the God of plan and order. Let Your unction be upon my mind to function for knowledge, wisdom, and understanding, for planning, visioning, and strategizing that my days ahead will be in order and in line with Your plan and purpose. I may not see the whole thing but please guide me one step at a time. My plans are still subject to Your change and revision. I abide in You; please let Your words abide in me so You may direct my path. In You and through You I can be bold, courageous, and confident because my life is in Your Hand, dear Lord Jesus I pray, Amen.

Reflective Questions

1. Have you been in a state of expectation or anticipation?

   _____

   _____

   _____

2. What do you do every first month of the year? Why?

   _____

   _____

   _____

3. Do you believe in New Year's resolution? If yes, why? If not, why?

   _____

   _____

   _____

4. How do you exercise faith in planning?

   _____

   _____

   _____

LAMENT

so here i am.
an island on a vast ocean
amongst the high-rushing waves
the mutiny and the mockery of the sea.
i am a house sans a roof
a tree sans leaves
a bird sans wings
in a desert of moroseness.
yes, I'm alive, but
like a mem'ry ling'ring hauntingly.
you live for something
and I, for nothing
you sleep in smiles
i do in tears.
like a frozen corpse
in an autumn-like summer.
still a void, still an island
a wingless bird, a leafless tree
searching unfulfilled…
must this forever be?
A poem written 1972 by: Rebecca Ducil

CHAPTER 6
THE FATAL BLOW

"In the resurrection scheme of things, this has to happen: everything perishable taken off the shelves and replaced by the imperishable, this mortal replaced by the immortal. Then the saying will come true: Death swallowed by triumphant Life! Who got the last word, oh, Death? Oh, Death, who's afraid of you now?"
1 Corinthians 15:53-55 (MSG)

The 15-day prayer and fasting was extended. I had decided to continue until the end of the month, January 31, 2010. However, something happened during the last week. In the morning of January 28, I attended a ministers meeting. Before it ended, I was starting to feel weak as if having colds or fever. When I got back home in the afternoon, I rested hoping I would feel better. In the evening, I still felt the same. The most important thing I did that day since the time my strength was failing was to pray.

> *"God is our refuge and strength, an ever-present help in trouble."* Psalm 46:1(NIV)

> *"Then they cried to the Lord in their trouble, and He saved them from their distress."* Psalm 107:13 (NIV)

God is alive. He is everywhere. I can call on Him anywhere, anytime, and whatever situation. Softly, I muttered and whispered to God my agony.

Until evening, my hope and peace were expressed in prayers intermittently between sleep and simply resting in bed. I took additional vitamin C and drank lots of water to give me strength and resistance. I tried to sleep in the evening hoping my blood pressure would slow down. Yet, it didn't. So, I checked my blood pressure. No wonder I had been feeling weak the whole day! It continued to go higher as the evening got late. When my blood pressure monitor went EE (double error reflected from Omron blood pressure monitor when the blood pressure is so high, more than 200), I was alarmed. That was almost midnight. I quickly said to my husband, "I need to go to the ER." My last resort was to go to the hospital. Once there, we waited for several hours.

In the emergency department, I went through all the process, the usual standard procedures. How I wished I could say, "Can't you see my blood pressure is high? Why can't you give me something to lower it ASAP (as soon as possible)?" Didn't they know the adverse effect of prolonged high blood pressure? I couldn't do anything but follow instructions and kept quiet. I was getting weaker and weaker, feeling tired and exhausted. Thank God, my husband was not barred from sitting beside me all through the process. I sat close beside him, intertwined my arm with his arm, and leaned on his shoulder while waiting for my name to be called.

Until when will I wait? What will be the next step? How many times will they take my vital signs – in the same room aside from those taken during the first and succeeding steps? Still holding my husband's arm and leaning my head on his shoulder, I continued to pray quietly.

"God, please heal me, please take control of my situation. I believe You're here with me and won't leave me alone. You are my Healer, my Deliverer, my Protector, my Shield, my Great Physician. My strength

is in You, my life is in You. You are my life. Glorify Your name in this life."

I softly hummed melodies of praise and worship. Even just the thought of the tune and lyrics of worship songs rested my mind, calmed my soul, and soothed my spirit. I was connecting with Him and I believed He surely listened with delight.

Prayers, worship, and God's Word made alive in my mind and heart gave me physical strength and assurance with peace beyond human understanding. In my personal relationship with God, those disciplines were instrumental in giving me peace that counteracted doubt, worry, or fear.

"Even though I walk through the valley of the shadow of death, I will fear no evil, for You are with me; Your rod and Your staff, they comfort me." Psalm 23:4 NIV

"So do not fear, for I am with you; do not be dismayed, for I am your God. I will strengthen you and help you; I will uphold you with my righteous right hand." Isaiah 41:10 NIV

Those verses ran spontaneously, swiftly through my mind. I believe the Holy Spirit reminded me of what was deposited within my spirit at the most appropriate time of my urgent need. I believe Jesus' words in John 6:63,

"The Spirit gives life, the flesh counts for nothing. The words I have spoken to you are spirit and they are life" NIV.

I reiterated Peter's reply to Jesus in John 6:68,

"Lord, to whom shall we go? You have the words of eternal life" NIV.

I ran to the name above every name, strong as a tower; there I am safe (Proverbs 18:10). The name is Jesus, none else.

Jesus… Jesus… in Jesus' name… in Jesus' name. I didn't know anymore what to pray but simply utter His name. "Take over… take charge… Lord Jesus."

Still waiting for my name to be called again, I attempted to transfer to the seat across from me. It was just a few steps away. I rose from my seat and with my husband helping to hold me up, I plodded. When I was almost to my goal and ready to sit down,

I vomited. Just a little sticky liquid poured out from my mouth. Then I fainted. It was about 4:30 a.m. I did not regain consciousness, and to this day do not know what happened next. My memory was totally gone.

According to my husband's recollection, a sequence of rapid actions followed thereafter in the emergency's waiting room, in the emergency room, and then in the ICU in those times of my ordeal. From his narration, I can visualize a TV or movie scene in a hospital where the rush-hush commotion of the medical staff fills the screen. Urgent action, suspense, and drama to save and heal must have dominated the atmosphere.

My husband recalled that thirty minutes after I passed out, the hospital staff attended to me. I was placed in a wheelchair and a doctor was available. I was in an unconscious state as blood tests were conducted. Though my eyes were open wide, I couldn't recognize my environment. *How could I when I became unconscious?* Thereafter, I was transferred to an emergency room. There, my clothes were changed for a hospital gown and I was laid down in bed. It was already 6:00 a.m. I still couldn't distinguish nor recognize my surrounding or any person around me. But I spoke, my husband continued his narration. I kept saying, "Don't leave me." Why did I say those words?

The Fatal Blow

I believe it was not a sense of his presence, much more seeing him physically though my eyes were opened, but because my last memory was that he was holding my arm before I passed out. Before I fainted, I was also praying for God not to leave me alone.

Several tests were conducted again to identify the cause of my fainting other than my accelerated blood pressure. At 6:30 a.m., my husband left to go home to sleep a little. He was deprived of sleep all throughout the evening until that time. He began to feel groggy. He came back to the hospital and waited for the result. Then, he was informed of the decision. I was to be transferred to the Intensive Care Unit in the afternoon because my condition was deteriorating. I was totally unconscious. My husband took the initiative to ask the doctor about my condition. The doctor replied that in her five years experience in the emergency, there was only 45-50% chance of survival for those who were afflicted with hyponatremia[1]. It is a condition of the body having low salt below the normal requirement which is 135 to 145. Below 135 or above 145 would be irregular and cause harm to the body. My sodium went down to 111, 24 below the body's requirement. It was very low. It is a rare malady and those who survive could possibly become vegetated.

No longer will the person recover the normal life he/she used to have. He/she will require care and assistance for everything as long as he/she lives.

My husband went out of the emergency room. He stayed outside, sat down, wanting to clear his mind. He felt numbed by the shock of what was happening. He had his share of trauma, too. That Friday was no doubt his saddest day because he witnessed firsthand the critical condition and ordeal I went through. I was already in a coma. If ever I awakened, there was no assurance I would live normally the rest of my life. Uncertainties were compounded and led to other distressing anxieties. I could also imagine him facing the dim reality that he could have lost me. He confided to me later that during those times, he asked himself, "Can we just die at the same time?" He was also confronted with questions like how could he live life taking care of an invalid spouse. We were already struggling financially; an additional death-like or near death or long-term health crisis was beyond his capacity to handle.

Later in the ICU (Intensive Care Unit), my medical condition was already identified. There I was closely monitored. Salt was slowly introduced to my body. Improvements were observed in the succeeding days. The first brain activities noticed were when my eyes were opened partially, then closed again soon, and continued sleeping. Then, I began to recover my ability to speak, but the words referred to my high school days in my hometown. They noticed my memory coming back when words came out of my mouth again. My husband recognized that they were still about the past, many years ago, but later than the high school days. He knew because we were schoolmates during our mid-teen years and continued to be friends in our late teens until we finally got married. My body was in the present, but my mind was in the past. I was still in a sleeping state.

My son visited me at the emergency as well as in the ICU. My one and only daughter, Revena, flew from another city and arrived Monday evening to visit, and stayed until a day after I was released from the hospital. My sister, Masing, who is also living in another city, visited me when she came to know about my serious condition. Minister friends visited too and prayed for me. Visitors were only allowed into the ICU two by two. After I regained consciousness, my husband told me who had come to see me. I also came to know after I recovered, that a deluge of prayers and intercessions from fellow ministers and friends in America and in the Philippines stormed the heavens for my behalf.

Wednesday afternoon, February three, I woke up. Finally, I fully recovered consciousness. I saw the gadgets, the life-saving devices, connected to several parts of my body. I looked around me and that was all I can do. I didn't have the strength to do otherwise. Then, I looked farther. I could see from the narrow opening of the dividing curtain in front of me. I saw two people at the nurse station. In that small room, I experienced for the first time in my whole life how it was in an ICU. I wanted to ask the purpose for those medical equipment attached to my body, but I couldn't. To remain lying down... still and calm in bed was the best thing to do; to lift my hand, or lower arm, or even to utter a word was much effort. Enough that I was conscious again and can see my surrounding, for that moment at least.

My daughter revealed that when she visited me in the ICU and came to know my condition, she planned to prepare for any eventuality like a casket, a funeral service, or any of those sorts. I understand her because she is a nurse who has several years of work experience in the ICU. She knew the seriousness of my condition. She is a brave and practical young woman like her father, but now her father's practical wisdom had turned into an "I don't know, I don't know what to do" rock bottom. I thank God that when my husband's inner strength was stretched to the limit, my daughter, the eldest among my children, stood strong.

I recall that the only times I was in the hospital were when I delivered my daughter and two sons. I am petite, but was never sickly. As a woman in ministry in the Philippines and in the US, many times I was requested to visit and pray for patients in the hospital and in the ICU too. That time, it seems, was my turn to experience personally how it was to be hospitalized and to be in an ICU. Now, I can visit and pray for people with greater empathy and deeper compassion.

I was transferred to a regular room. There, I began to eat a regular diet, to rise up with assistance then eventually on my own. I also started to walk, at first with assistance or being watched closely, and then walk on my own few steps at a time, until I was able to walk to the bathroom, then around the room. The second time I was in the bathroom, I suddenly fell down. Nobody was around, no nurse, or nurse assistant, or anybody from the nurse station. My daughter wasn't there too because she has not yet arrived at the hospital from our residence. My strength waned, my eyesight dimmed, and I felt dizzy. I couldn't rise up. The only one thing I could was pray. I was thankful my head did not hit the toilet bowl. Thank God, a nurse came later and saw me lying on the floor in the bathroom.

"What happened?" She uttered showing concern and helped me rise up and get back to my bed.

I stayed for another day in the hospital. With medications and regular diet, I gradually gained a little strength to walk outside my room and back to my bed. Those were attempts to normalize my body movements. A couple visited me. It was such a comfort and joy to receive a gift from them, a flowering plant. They didn't know anthurium is my favorite flower.

On my last day, I received a call. It was from an elder of an American Indian church who invited me to speak for a Sunday morning service. He reminded me of the coming schedule. The invitation was a month ago and they didn't have any idea what happened to me.

"Oh, I'm sorry. Right now, I'm still in the hospital," I replied. Graciously, he rescheduled my preaching commitment to the following month.

Finally, on February five, I received the good news that I was to be released from the hospital. I can't fully describe my exact feelings... beyond words... can't find words... just thankful. After complying with all the requirements, which my husband accomplished by going through all the tedious process, my daughter

The Fatal Blow

and son helped me get ready to leave. At last, my husband finished everything in the hospital office and in the pharmacy for my medicines. We left the hospital around 9:00 p.m. It was also late evening when my husband and I went to the emergency department that fateful evening of Thursday, January 28.

The eight days of ordeal was over. Sans my first son who was in our country of origin, my family celebrated quietly with a late dinner in a Thai restaurant just before it closed. Only then, we felt our belly's starving. I sipped the warm broth of the seafood soup and savored the fish and vegetables. At last, I enjoyed a gourmet meal that was appropriate for both my palate and nutrition. Two days after, we dined again in the same restaurant. We had to, because nobody seemed to care for cooking; all concerns were centered on me. Being together seldom happens; we must seize the moment and enjoy every bit of it.

My daughter quipped, "This is my birthday treat," as she prepared to pay the bill.

It was a double celebration because it was the eve of my daughter's birthday. With the healthful, sumptuous food before me, miracle healing, life extended, and my family together with me, I can hear my Heavenly Father saying, "Taste and see that the Lord is good" (Psalm 34:8a NLT/NIV).

Let's Pray Together

*"I also tell you this:
If two of you agree down here on earth concerning
anything you ask, my Father in heaven
will do it for you."* NLT
Matthew 18:19

Gracious Lord,
Thank You for extending my borrowed life. Words are not enough to fully express my gratitude. When I look back, all I can say is "Thank You" and nothing at all. A mountain wave of emotions engulfs me and I just sigh. My tears keep rolling down my cheeks in amazement to Your marvelous works for me. You showered me with Your love and care during those times of helplessness and hopelessness. Your Presence with authority and control was all over me and the people around me those days. Thank You, my Creator, my Lifegiver, my God. You are true to Your word, " . . . I am with you and will keep you . . ." (Genesis 28:15a NKJV/NASB). *You held me in the hollow of Your Hand and I was safe all the way. Truly, nothing is difficult for You and what is impossible for man is possible for You. This monument of miracle cannot be forgotten. This is life changing, life transforming. I am never the same*

again. Only You, Oh Lord, can do this. It is You who give life, it is You who can take it, whenever, wherever, however. You are still the supreme ruler of life. To You belong the glory and praises; I pray in Jesus' name who is the way, the truth, and the life, Amen.

Reflective Questions

1. How would you feel when something you don't want to happen, whatever it may be, comes to reality?

   _____

   _____

2. Do you prepare to caution yourself against health issues or life threatening conditions and cushion the adverse effect thereafter?

   _____

   _____

3. How do you face the truth about death?

   _____

   _____

4. Was there someone in your family or a relative who became ill or seriously sick in the hospital? How did you feel? What did you do?

   _____

   _____

   _____

PART III

THE AFTERMATH – WHAT NOW, MY LORD?

THEN

*"Be strong. Take courage. Don't be intimidated.
Don't give them a second thought because God,
your God, is striding ahead of you.
He's right there with you. He won't let you down;
He won't leave you."*
Deuteronomy 31:6 (MSG)

Still with meager strength, I attended church that Sunday with my husband, daughter, and son. What a blessed day to start life anew! I felt a sense of strangeness. The surroundings seemed new to me as if I was in a new place. In the church, I didn't immediately recognize the people. They seemed to be familiar, but not really. Everything seemed new to me as if I had not been there or had not seen the people for ages... as if I was in another space and time. I also noticed this as I looked out the car's window as my husband drove home. There was a general sense of cleanliness, peace, quiet, and orderliness without a trace of the highly urbanized, messy, dirty environment.

The people in the apartment building appeared unfamiliar too. It seemed strange. Was it because my body was at rest for a long time, disconnected with the outside world around me? I don't know, I can't understand. All that matters was that I was grateful I was alive and well again.

Days passed. I rested, slept, and ate choice nutritious food. I moved around slowly and lay down again. That was my daily routine to regain strength and fully recover. I could read my Bible for a limited time, a little here and a little there. My eyes got tired easily and my head got dizzy soon. My recourse was to watch TV and listen to spiritual shows for short periods of time. I would listen more than watch in order to take care of my eyes and head.

A couple of weeks after my hospital discharge I received a phone call from Pastor Allen Castro of Heart of Worship in the City of Industry. He told me that they had been praying for me as their church anniversary speaker. After they heard of what happened to me, he called to ask if I could speak on the last Sunday of the month. That would be barely a month after I left the hospital. I was not sure I would be strong enough to stand so long and to speak for 45 minutes. I would not be just speaking, I would be preaching.

"I'll pray about it and call you before the weekend." I replied.

Every time before I commit myself to preach, I seek God's guidance and anointing. I'm wary of my position as His mouthpiece, my incapacity without Him, and the power of His spoken Word.

Will I say yes to the invitation as for self-aggrandizement, or to spread the blessing of God's Word? In my physical weakness, God could take over and receive all the glory. God did not extend my life for nothing.

> "... *the life which I now live in the flesh I live by faith in the Son of God, who loved me and gave Him*self for me" (Gal. 2:20b NKJV).

This was my life verse in the 1990's. Now it has blossomed with deeper hues and glistening texture like a full blown flower. Life has embraced the deeper meaning, distinct focus, and bright tomorrow. Life has become more LIFE to me with this taste of the resurrection power of Jesus infused into my life. How could you deny this reality and this truth more than physical existence? As apostle Paul considered himself crucified with Christ Jesus, so do I. Not only was I dead to sin but I was in a death-like condition for six days in the ICU without certainty of full recovery.

The pastor was happy when I called to commit myself for their church anniversary. I am not concerned with impressing God and other people with my gift of speaking or knowledge of the Bible, nor with appearing righteous and gaining favor. What gains pre-eminence is obedience to His plan and direction in the new chapter of my life.

During those days of resting something happened. It was something I didn't expect because the tranquility of my aloneness in the apartment was good enough an excuse for me to find rest. I was sitting down near the dining table when suddenly an impression came to my mind – Psalm 118:17. Slowly, my frail body reached for my Bible to read the text from different versions,

"I shall not die but live and declare/proclaim/ tell the works and recount the illustrious/brilliantly outstanding acts/deeds of the Lord."

I felt the warmth all over me, I felt life. I could sense His Presence. He was speaking; I knew when He was speaking to my spirit. It was clear, distinct, and profound. His voice is not audible but you know when you know... that you know. His Presence is amazing, indescribable, and undeniable.

I was speechless. In quiet, humble adoration I bowed down in tears to the awesome God. A few more days passed and the word of the Lord came again. This time He did not show me where to find the verse but spoke in a soft still voice,

> *"You anoint my head with oil, my cup runs over."* (NKJV)

I'm familiar with this verse in Psalm 23:5b. The Holy Spirit was speaking to me again. I believe this time was to confirm that God healed me; He performed His healing miracle in my brain. Biblically, one of the uses of oil is for healing. *Oh, my Lifegiver, my Great Physician was in His wondrous acts of restoration again.* He breathed life into my immobile body in the ICU. That was a time and place for my resting, refreshing, and restoration.

THEN

The Lord knew how my life was battered and tired with the battles in life from all sides and areas – personal, family, and ministry. My soul – mind, will, and emotion – needed rest and it could rest only in Jesus, the anchor. Jesus is the God of restoration. Jesus conquered death through His resurrection. His resurrection made it possible for every faculty of my mortal body to be quickened and slowly come back to normal. *What for?* Many hyponathremia patients did not fully recover. There are those who have recovered but are incapacitated the rest of their lives. Not for me! His life for me is to declare His works. His purpose will be my purpose. Here I was, in less than a month after my life threatening experience; I would be speaking and was scheduled to speak again in the following month in another city. In the deep recesses of my being, my spirit sang, *In Him I live and move and have my being* as in Acts 17:28a (KJV/NIV) . . . *what a mighty God I serve!*[1]

CHAPTER 7
STAND FIRM

"But Moses answered the people, 'Do not be afraid. Stand firm and you will see the deliverance the Lord will bring you today. The Egyptians you see today you will never see again.'"

Exodus 14:13 NIV

Let me share with you about my preaching on "Stand Firm, Be Still, Move On" based on Exodus 14:13-15. I found this passage gravitating after the deadly battle I went through. Each verse served as a guide what to do thereafter. Also, it became a source of comfort, strength, and courage to move on with life.

The background of the story can be found in Exodus 13:17-18a,

"When the Pharaoh let the people go, God did not lead them on the road through the Philistine country, though that was shorter. For God said, 'if they face war, they might change their minds and return to Egypt.' So, God led the people around by the desert road toward the Red Sea." NIV

Exodus 13:20-22 says,
"After leaving Succoth, they camped at Etham on the edge of the desert. (Succoth is the place where they camped after they left Egypt – Numbers 33:5-6) *By day the Lord went ahead of them in a pillar of cloud to guide them on their way and by night in a pillar of fire to give them light, so that they could travel by day or night. Neither the pillar of cloud by day nor the pillar of fire by night left its place in front of the people."* NIV

Chapter 14:1-15 says,
"Then the Lord said to Moses, 'Tell the Israelites to turn back and encamp near Pi Hahiroth, between Migdol and the sea. They are to encamp by the sea, directly opposite Baal

Zephon. Pharaoh will think, The Israelites are wandering around the land in confusion, hemmed in by the desert. And I will harden Pharaoh's heart, and he will pursue them. But I will gain glory for myself through Pharaoh and all his army, and the Egyptians will know that I am the Lord.' So the Israelites did this.

When the king of Egypt was told that the people had fled, Pharaoh and his officials changed their minds about them and said, 'What have we done? We have let the Israelites go and have lost their services!' So he had his chariot made ready and took his army with him. He took 600 of the best chariots, along with all the other chariots of Egypt, with officers over all of them. The Lord hardened the heart of Pharaoh King of Egypt, so that he pursued the Israelites, who were marching out boldly. The Egyptians – all Pharaoh's horses and chariots, horsemen and troops – pursued the Israelites and overtook them as they camped by the sea near Pi Hahiroth, opposite Baal Zephon.

As Pharaoh approached, the Israelites looked up, and there were the Egyptians, marching after them. They were terrified and cried out to the Lord. They said to Moses, 'Was it because there were no more graves in Egypt that you brought us to the desert to die? What have you done to us by bringing us out of Egypt? Didn't we say to you in Egypt, 'Leave us alone; let us serve the Egyptians'? It would have been better for us to serve the Egyptians than to die in the desert!'" NIV

This is the story about the Israelites before crossing the Red Sea. We can see in the story that after the death of the first born in Egypt including the son of Pharaoh, the Israelites were released to leave Egypt. God was in control of the whole situation. God was leading them to move around the desert road toward the Red Sea, His pillar of cloud by day and pillar of fire by night, His instruction to turn back and encamp between Migdol and the sea, and His hardening of Pharaoh's heart again. He knew the thoughts and intents of the people in both camps. He could see the whole picture, the "before-during-after" of the whole situation. But the Israelites didn't. God knew what was best for His people. When there was deliverance, they agreed, but when there was danger, they blamed Moses. That's what they did when they saw the approaching Egyptian army. Their first and immediate response was to panic and be terrified, blaming, and accusing Moses. They totally forgot all God's miraculous ways of saving them, protecting them, providing them, and leading them. Despite the accusation, Moses exhibited an opposite response. It was not an eye for an eye reply, or anger, or rebuke. He gave three instructions to counteract fear of the enemy.

Moses told them to, first of all, stand firm – to stand and not fall down with diminishing strength, to stand and not sway around to turn back where they left behind, nor sway around to face other people to blame and accuse. It should be a firm stand, immoveable by any sudden, unexpected turn of events. It should be a firm stand on solid ground to be able to walk and not sink down. It should be a firm stand on the solid ground of faith in God with whom they had a relationship as His children and chosen people.

1 Samuel 6:20 says

"Who is able to stand before the Lord (ESV)
"Who can stand in the presence of the Lord, this holy God?" (NIV)

The presence of the Lord was with the Israelites as manifested by the pillar of cloud by day and pillar of fire by night. Proverbs 12:7 says,

". . . but the house of the righteous stands firm." (NIV)

How will the righteous stand firm? The instruction in 2 Chronicles 20:17 was

". . . Take up your positions; stand firm and see the deliverance the Lord will give you. . ." (NIV)

We can stand firm if we know our position – our identity in Christ whose redeeming blood made us children of the living God, of the most High God.
Psalm 22:23 says,

"You who fear the Lord, praise Him! All you offspring of Jacob, glorify Him, and stand in awe of him, all you offspring of Israel!" (ESV)

Fear of the enemy will immobilize and destroy you, but fear of God will deliver and preserve you. Reverential fear of God will lead you to praise Him and stand in awe of Him. He was, He is, and will always be. Yes, human frailty will cause us to fear but you can overcome fear with the personal knowledge of who He is, your identity with Him, and what He did in the past. It wasn't long enough for Israelites to forget what God has done for them. They could have overcome fear by standing in awe of His reality and praise Him. Yes, the enemy is real and powerful before their eyes at that moment, but God is real too and more powerful than the enemy. Whose power will you abide, the power against you, or the power for and with you?

> *"Therefore, my dear brothers, stand firm. Let nothing move you. Always give yourselves fully to the work of the Lord, because you know that your labor in the Lord is not in vain."* (NIV) *"Therefore, my beloved brothers, be steadfast, immovable* (stand firm – not soon shaken), *always abounding in the work of the Lord knowing that in the Lord your labor is not in vain."* 1 Corinthians 15:58 (ESV)

What is the result of standing firm? "You will see the deliverance the Lord will bring you today," not tomorrow, not later, but today – now - at the very point and time of need. Then you will not see the enemy again, no more terror, no more panic, no more intimidation, no more fear for the mighty Hand of God will wipe out and annihilate the enemy. The people of God should stand firm on solid ground to walk even in the shadow of the valley of death, in the shadow of taunting terror and fear. Why? Because the solid ground on which we stand firm is the truth that He will never neither leave us nor forsake us. He is our Jehovah Nissi[1], our banner, our protection, our victory. The truth will set us free from fear and intimidation of the enemy.

For us today, the truth is the foundation of the church of Jesus Christ who said

". . . upon this rock I will build my church, and all the powers of hell will not conquer it" (Matthew 16:18 NLT).

You and I who receive the atoning sacrifice and redeeming grace of Christ Jesus are that church. That is the solid ground where we can stand firm today. We should not allow the enemy to dislodge us from our position in Christ Jesus, nor negate our identity as children of the living God, or to captivate us to former bondage. We will see God's deliverance before our eyes and not the enemy. He will change our focus. We will see God in all that He is and never to see the enemy again. Either He will annihilate the enemy or remove the enemy from our sight so that our focus on God will not have any obstruction.

Let's Pray Together

"I also tell you this:
If two of you agree down here on earth concerning
anything you ask, my Father in heaven
will do it for you." NLT
Matthew 18:19

Gracious Lord,
Thank You for the strength You give me from day to day. Your strength never wanes, but rather increases as I need it more or when my strength is failing. You don't want me to faint nor stumble. Thank You for such love, care, and concern. As Your child by virtue of the blood of Jesus, my Savior, I can stand firm for my identity is in Christ Jesus. Such identity is my position and my possession; no one and nothing can dislodge me from this position as a child of the King, no one can grab my possession of salvation as well as my inheritance which is heaven. I'll take hold of my position and stand on solid ground of the Rock of all ages with the power of the Holy Spirit, that I may be able to stand firm on solid ground against the wiles and schemes of the devil. My strength is heavily anchored in Christ Jesus, the Word made flesh, I won't be swayed to the left nor to the right but stand straight with head held up high to the One from where comes my help, the One who made heaven and earth. This I declare and pray in the mighty name of Jesus, Amen.

Reflective Questions

1. Was there a time in your spiritual walk when your strength was failing? How did it happen and how did you recover?

   _____

   _____

2. What factors caused your spiritual weakening. Who/what were instrumental towards your recovery or restoration?

   _____

   _____

3. What lessons have you learned in the/those experience/experiences?

   _____

   _____

4. Are you willing to share your experience of God's enabling strength to others?

   _____

   _____

CHAPTER 8
BE STILL

"The Lord will fight for you; you need only to be still."
Exodus 14:14 NIV

After standing firm in a sure foundation and in solid ground, the next thing to do is to be still. This instruction was for the Israelites not to do anything. To do nothing does not mean the absence of physical activity, but the absence of striving, of resisting, of struggling, of proving, of grumbling, of making excuses, and so on and so forth of a lot more except being still. Be still. Just be quiet and trust God to do His work. In their situation, the Israelites became panicky; they were immediately in commotion. The first thing they did was to accuse and blame Moses. The devil is the accuser of the brethren. His devise is to divide and conquer. You know what you can do and what you can't do, but God can do. Trust the person whom you have established your relationship with. Trust God who is a person, not a thing, not a philosophy, not a religion, or an institution for "The Lord will fight for you." Moses did not say "The Lord will fight with you," but "for you." They didn't have any participation in the fight. No need for cooperation or partnership.

"Is anything too hard for the Lord?" Genesis 18:14a KJV/NIV/NLT.

The people of God cannot be still because their tendency is to trust in themselves or the world around them, but not God. It is in being still wherein we will know that God is God, when we let God be God, when we let Him do His ways. God knows and wants the best for us. To be still is to be in quietness and trust, in full assurance. Any attempt to do otherwise is futile. The Exodus 14 situation shows that the enemy is very near them and their arms are no match to the Egyptian army.

Exodus 13:18b NIV—*"The Israelites went up out of Egypt armed for battle."*

Exodus 14:7 NIV – *"He (Pharaoh) took 600 of the best chariots, along with all the other chariots of Egypt, with officers over all of them."*

Psalm 46:10 NIV – *"Be still and know that I am God; I will be exalted among the nations, I will be exalted in the earth."*

The command for the Israelites to be still is to cease from striving and exalt God on earth among the nations. It was necessary for them to be in that alarming situation for God to show Himself who He is. Instead of setting their attention on God, praising Him and exalting Him, they wrestled and fought with Moses and resisted God's ways. The command was to be still, stop depending on themselves, on their own ways, and on their own understanding. Pride and arrogance in their heart caused them not to submit, but insisted in their haughty and independent spirit.

". . . Leave us alone . . . It would have been better for us to serve the Egyptians than to die in the desert!" (Exodus 14:12 NIV)

How many of us today are consciously or unconsciously telling God "Leave us alone?"

Let's Pray Together

*"I also tell you this:
If two of you agree down here on earth concerning
anything you ask, my Father in heaven
will do it for you."* NLT
Matthew 18:19

Gracious Lord,
Thank You for the liberty and privilege to enter into Your Presence. There, I will be still and know that You are God. In Your Presence there is fullness of joy beyond words can say and peace that overwhelm all understanding. Your Presence is more than enough, more than enough for me. I can be still, be quiet, and bask in how great You are. I can forget my sorrow, for You will turn them into dancing. I can forget my worries, for You will turn them into joy. I can forget my fears, for You will turn them into feats. I can forget my travails, for You can turn them into triumphs. Thank You Lord for Your grace of stillness, making me immoveable, unshaken, undaunted by the works of the enemy. The knowledge of who You are and that You are my God and my Heavenly Father makes me still. I can be still in sweet surrender to

Your impossible ways; I behold their unfolding before my eyes in the presence of my enemies. The devil and demons tremble at Your name Lord Jesus; their works are vanquished and vanished. I will be still and witness Your mighty works for my behalf. I will be silent in reverence to Your work in my life. I will bow down to Your lordship, dear Jesus, Amen.

Reflective Questions

1. Is finding time to be still before God a struggle or a delight, a dread or a desire?

2. What do you expect when you spend time with God?

3. Does stillness before God happen only in secluded prayer times? If yes, why? If no, why?

CHAPTER 9

MOVE ON

"Then the Lord said to Moses, 'Why are you crying out to me? Tell the Israelites to move on.'"
Exodus 14:15 NIV

The third instruction of God through Moses was for the Israelites to move on. They needed to continue in their journey after being still, in quiet assurance and confidence in God. They should not turn back or remain stagnant, immobilized by fear, but should move on. They were instructed to be still in order to stop doing something which is resistance against God and to move on in order to do something which is to continue the journey. Their moving on was a step of faith and obedience so that the miracle would be in operation. God told Moses in verse 16

"Raise your staff and stretch out your hand over the sea to divide the water so that the Israelites can go through the sea on dry ground" (NIV).

God instructed the Israelites to move on first before instructing Moses what to do. The Lord Jesus said to Thomas in John 20:29b

"Because you have seen me, you have believed; blessed are those who have not seen and yet have believed" (NIV).

The Israelites needed to move on to test, exercise, and substantiate their faith on what they had not yet seen but hoped for – God's present mighty act of deliverance. There was no more time to wait and see God act first before they moved on. By force of circumstances, they had no option but to move on at God's command or else face the enemy and die. They were not to move on to be paralyzed, but to make a step forward.

Without moving on they wouldn't be able to go through on dry ground. To move on by faith is to open the door of miracles, to see what they have not known or seen before (Jeremiah 33:3), and to experience the immeasurable act beyond their thoughts or imagination (Ephesians 3:20). To move on by faith commences the departure of the sea of turmoil, hindrance, difficulty, so that God's children can continue moving forward. They needed to move on in order to go through. The sea of hindrances will give way for the children of the Creator of the universe and King of kings to walk safely on dry ground.

We too, should act first by moving without doubt, hesitation, and reservation. Our faith is not with ifs and buts. Otherwise, it is not faith at all. It is not conditional for God to act first or show signs of confirmation. Our act of faith by moving on pleases God and prompts Him to make possible what is impossible for us.

Shall we remain in apathy and lose faith because of stumbling blocks of various kinds at different times? Should we walk in lethargy because of repeated or successive failures or in anxiety because of waning hope; or shall we move on to continue life's journey with a relationship with God, fighting the good fight of faith as apostle Paul said?

I ended my preaching at the City of Industry with this challenge. As the Israelites crossed the Red Sea by following the instructions to stand firm, be still, and move on, we too, today, can cross the sea of challenges we face in life by following the same instructions. With Christ we can wave high the banner of victory; without Christ, defeat and death follow. This challenge is for you, too.

The first thing I did when I got home from the preaching commitment was to lie down and rest till the end of the day. I needed to recover the strength used up in standing for about 45 minutes, speaking, expounding, stressing points, and praying. Without the Holy Spirit's anointing, my physical body as His vessel couldn't deliver His message during that early time of my recovery. My frail body was drained of physical exertion and it was wise to take care of it because I am not my own. I am a temple of the Holy Spirit, God's property, and accountable to God the owner.

A month passed by. Recovery continued as I started to slowly move around doing light chores and reading more for exercise of both body and mind. Then, the postponed preaching schedule at an American Indian church came. That was the last week of the month, in time for the Palm Sunday. That time, I regained the energy to speak and preach twice in a day, for Sunday morning and evening services. It was followed by a Wednesday midweek service. I was amazed and am still amazed with what had been happening to me. God was showing me and my world that He was able, always able for me. In my weakness, He was my strength; in my incapacity, He was my enabler. It's all because He is my healer, restorer, and sustainer and He can be that to you also. My strength is in the Lord who made heaven and earth, and me as well. He gave me the gift of speaking so He could make me use it even in times of difficulty. He will provide where I lack in every opportunity. He is my sufficiency.

On the third month, I was able to move around with increased stamina. I tried to walk within the apartment building; so, I took the chance by inviting some of my neighbors for a testimony gathering. *Yes, that is a good idea! Why not?* True it was. They were curious to know what happened to me. I was excited. While still fresh, I should share and let others know what the Lord had done. Miracles are not confined to the historical past, but they continue to this day and always will be, as long as there's a need and there's faith to believe.

Since we were new in the apartment, it was also a time of getting to know each other. After hellos and exchanging pleasantries, I started to narrate. Everybody was all ears to listen until the end. From this simple, small get together, a Bible study was birthed. I decided to move on in any way I could. I didn't have the strength yet to resume my other home Bible studies; but, it was good enough to move on with my teaching ministry at least with one Bible study.

Let's Pray Together

"I also tell you this:
If two of you agree down here on earth concerning
anything you ask, my Father in heaven
will do it for you." NLT
Matthew 18:19

Gracious Lord,
Thank You for the strength and energy You give me in order to move on. With Your promise, that You will teach me and guide me in the way that I should go (Psalm 32:8); I am rest assured that You will remove the rough road ahead of me. Because of You and Your unfailing faithfulness, I can go on. I could move forward with confidence that everything will be all right. You will never leave me alone on the road; You will not set me aside by the sideways, but keep me moving towards my destiny. On the pathway of Your direction, anoint me with Your wisdom, discernment, and courage to do Your works for You promised "he who believes in Me, the works that I do he will do also, and greater works than these he will do because I will go to My Father"(John 14:12 NKJV). As I continue on, with every day that You extend my borrowed

life, please bless me, so I can bless others because I cannot give what I do not have. All that I am, all that I have come from You. May they be sufficient to live a life that will bring glory to You in financial and material provisions and in spiritual enablement to use the gifts You gave for the furtherance of the gospel of Christ, expansion of Your Kingdom on earth as it is in heaven; in Jesus' name I pray, Amen.

Reflective Questions

1. What transitions have you encountered in your life? Describe your experience/experiences, negative or positive.

   _____

   _____

2. Identify the things you need to leave behind and those you should bring along with you as you move on to the next chapter of your life.

   _____

   _____

3. Why do you think it is necessary and important to allow a transition period before any change?

   _____

   _____

4. Who, what contributed to your transition and helped you walk through it?

   _____

   _____

PART IV
THE RECOLLECTIONS – DANGERS AND TOILS

"Fear not, for I have redeemed you;
I have called you by your name;
You are Mine.

When you pass through the waters,
I will be with you;
And through the rivers, they shall not overflow you.
When you walk through the fire,
You shall not be burned,
Nor the flame scorch you.

For I am the Lord your God,
The Holy One of Israel, your Savior."
Isaiah 43:1b – 3a (NKJV)

"Do not be afraid, for I have ransomed you.
I have called you by name;
you are mine.

When you go through deep waters and great trouble,
I will be with you.
When you go through rivers of difficulty,
you will not drown!
When you walk through the fire of oppression,
you will not be burned up;
the flames will not consume you.

For I am the Lord, your God,
the Holy One of Israel, your Savior."
Isaiah 43:1b – 3a (NLT)

CHAPTER 10
ESCAPE FROM FIRE

At the onset of the millennium, negative anticipations crowded the minds of many people, even people of faith. Unfazed, I maintained my faith in God who is above the menace of the computer world. He promised a way of escape for His people.

My focus was to continue my commitment to serve God and my family. My travels in the first decade of the millennium were not confined to the Visayas islands (middle part of the Philippines) but included the national capital to attend retreats, conferences, or meetings with the Aglow national board along with my personal matters.

While on one of those travels, I saw a big billboard raised up high prominently along a busy boulevard in metropolitan Manila. It announced a convention to be conducted by the ministry of Don Clowers with Joyce Meyers as the main speaker. It was the first time Joyce Meyers had spoken in the Philippines, and the last. The convention was for pastors and leaders from all parts of the country with free accommodations, shuttle buses to and from the hotel and the venue, and lunch.

Since my stay was extended for personal concerns, I registered to attend. I was excited and thankful for the opportunity to attend a big convention and listen to a renowned Bible teacher. The fame of Joyce Meyers in the U.S. reached other nations including the Philippines. I didn't want to miss the opportunity to hear her speak in person without traveling overseas.

The coliseum was jam-packed. I didn't recognize anybody I knew, but I was enthralled with the atmosphere where everybody else seemed to know everybody. Aside from the congeniality, worship was awesome, like angelic voices of multitudes echoing through the huge coliseum. It was like heaven on earth.

Although I stayed with my relatives whenever I was in Manila, on the following day, I decided to stay in the hotel assigned to me. After our free lunch, we rode in the bus with an assigned number to our hotel. Far from my expectations, the room designated to me was crowded with mattresses. It was a low-cost hotel probably added to the list of accommodations for late registrants. I came to know later that others were assigned to better hotels. I wanted to leave, but I needed rest to be prepared for the evening service. Also, I didn't know how to commute from the hotel since I didn't reside in that city.

Thousands of conventioneers lined up for lunch meals. The time was consumed with lining up, eating, and riding the shuttle to the hotel and it took much of our afternoon. I just wanted to lie down and stretch my legs, but I slept. I must have been very tired. When I woke up, I was alone in the room. I rushed out and noticed the hurried steps of other people. The shuttle bus was about to leave. Gracious God! I woke up just in time. Carrying my purse, I had grabbed my small bag of belongings for a night's stay. I left nothing in the hotel. I had already decided not to go back there to give space for others, though the shuttle bus was a big help.

The evening session was as refreshing as the previous ones. There were special presentations too. The service ended at almost midnight. When we left the coliseum, it was raining. I was hungry and felt cold. The good thing was that I had brought an umbrella. I didn't know where the shuttle buses were parked. I tried to ride a jeepney (passenger jeep) to my relative's place, but there was none to their location. At about 12 midnight, jeepneys were rare. I decided to cross the other street headed to a restaurant that was still open, serving hot noodles and porridge. Anything would have been perfect for me. Since I was hungry, my tendency was to gulp the food. Afraid to upset my stomach, I satiated my appetite with soup that warmed my body.

It was still raining, but I had to find the shuttle bus going to our hotel. My attempt availed nothing. Though I decided earlier not to sleep in the hotel, it would be better than to be stranded under the rain in the middle of the night. I walked along the streets again, through non-stop rain. Though my umbrella was not big enough to shield me from the heavy rain, it was better than nothing. How I wished I had a raincoat. There I was in the same spot waiting for a jeepney I could ride to my niece's residence. It was past midnight. I was getting worried. I was afraid to ride a taxi alone at that time. At long last, the jeepney I had been waiting for came. When I arrived, my niece, Melody, was surprised, so I told her how it happened.

The following morning, I was on time at the coliseum. I didn't want to miss any part of the long service. Praise and worship began. I focused in my worship ignoring those around me. My audience is one, and only one, my Savior and Lord. What mattered to me was the privilege to commune and fellowship with God in such a rare environment. Greeting one another came next. Before we sat down, an announcement was given. Something of utmost concern had happened. Though I noticed a difference during the singing and a spirit of heaviness in the air, I had no inkling of what had happened that morning. One of the hotels had burned down. We needed to pray before proceeding. I muttered, "How sad." I looked around at the ponderous countenances of the audience. Sadness and gloom were evident. Some of the staff and volunteers were helping at the site and in the hospital. No wonder the praise and worship team had fewer singers and instrumentalists and were not as vibrant as before. When the name of the hotel and the location was mentioned, I was shocked. "I was there yesterday," I whispered. *I took a nap in the afternoon and planned to sleep in the night.* I recalled. The fire occurred past midnight, in the wee hours of the day. If my memory serves me right, numerous occupants were burned to death. I gasped, aghast in shock. *What if I found the shuttle and had slept there? I would have been one of the casualties.* I could have asked a thousand questions of "what ifs" but the reality was I was still alive.

I was awed with God's ways beyond my human comprehension. He knew it would happen; He is omniscient and omnipresent. I was in the very place of danger unaware of what would happen hours later – in less than 24 hours. Our human knowledge is limited. We do not know what a day may bring (Proverb 27:1). I can't grasp God's perfect ways to indemnify me from an impending danger. I can only bask in His love and care, on and on.

On the contrary how about those numerous conventioneers? They were ministers, pastors, and ministry leaders. Some were couples; some were with other family members, some with their church or ministry group. These verses cropped up in my mind for them:

"Precious in the sight of the Lord is the death of his saints" (Psalm 116:15 NIV).

"...to live is Christ and to die is gain" (Philippians 1:21 NIV).

I believe they were prepared to meet their God (Amos 4:12).

I can't remember anymore the number of people mentioned in the newspapers. Though the hotel was small, it was occupied by the conventioneers. There must have been many who passed away that day.

After receiving that day's free lunch, I found a place I could eat comfortably. Grateful for the messages I heard, I was comforted. Hours ago I'd been stupefied, unnerved, and disquieted from the appalling news. The consoling thought was that they met death when they were spiritually filled with songs and preaching of the Word.

My cell phone rang. I wondered if it might be my husband, my daughter, or either of my two sons? I heard the perturbed voice of the then Aglow national president in the Philippines, Rina Filart. "Where are you now? How are you?" She had heard the news and she knew I had attended the convention. She and the others on the national board were worried about me.

The tragedy filled the front page of the newspapers[1] that day. The names of the dead were listed. Many others were in the hospital fighting for life. My ministry friends, family, and relatives must have seen those gruesome pictures, too, and felt the same as I did. No matter how many questions were raised from all quarters of the country, the truth remained. They were dead.

Life is fleeting. Death comes to us anytime, anywhere, anyhow regardless of our religion, vocation, position, or education. Our physical life is temporary. Only the life that God gives is eternal.

After reading the newspaper, I sat down still stunned with what had happened that day. I could only imagine the busyness, the commotion, and the rush here and there to recover dead bodies, burned bodies, both whole and body parts, from the rubbles at the burned hotel. I envisioned the hurried steps and running of the medical people to and fro in the hospital, trying their best to save the dying. I didn't know what to do next. I lost the vibrancy I had gained during the prior days. I opted to sit down, relax, and comfort myself in the air-conditioned mall rather than beat the heat outside in the sunny afternoon to commute to my niece's apartment.

A few days after, I was home again, back with my family. Queries flooded my conversations with my family at home and among the church people, Aglow women, and fellow ministers at different occasions. Everybody who heard my story had the same reaction – gratefulness and praises to God for His wonderful ways to protect.

The rain and hunger that fateful midnight had been a blessing in disguise for me. *If it was indeed for me, what was it for those who died?* I opted to believe that

"...all things work together for good to them that love God, to them who are the called according to His purpose" (Romans 8:28 KJV).

Those things included the tragedy such as what they encountered. God can transform tragedy into triumph in sundry ways. The dead in Christ shall rise first at the voice of the archangel when the trumpet call of God sound (1 Thessalonians 4:16). For those who were burned and died, that was their last suffering. The fire was no match to the never ending lake of fire burning with brimstone or sulfur (Rev. 19:20). They graduated from their pain, sorrow, risk, struggle, sickness, and dangers of earthly life. It was a commencement flight from the uncertainties on earth swiftly into the certainty of heavenly bliss in the presence of God and Savior Jesus Christ for all eternity.

How about the bereaved family and friends? I can only imagine the shock, grief, and sorrow ineffable beyond expression. It is an acknowledged fact that death-related events such as the passing away of someone in the family, relative, or close friend is a common cause of stress. Most often, the closer the relationship, the deeper the sorrow becomes for the loss.

Part of the Filipino trait is for a traveler to bring goodies or souvenirs for family and friends when they return home. With their situation, these customs seem passé and nonsensical. What mattered was to receive the body of their loved one. No more, not a shadow but a coffin of burned body. Some could have received ashes or none at all, but only names. Cries and wails are inevitable. Maybe, some will simply sob to control their emotion, but unbearable pain within the crevices of their heart is scathingly deep that only the grace of God can alleviate and sustain.

The horror of death is intensified with this kind of death. We cannot choose how we die. If we could, we surely would want to escape the blazing heat of consuming fire. If we were in their shoes, what would have we done? Would we have imbued our sensibilities and judgments with condemnation by blaming the hotel, the convention organizers, ourselves, or God? Accusations will magnify the grief. We would rather be still and know that God is God (Psalm 46:10). He is sovereign. We better not duplicate the bigotry of

Job's friends but rather emulate Job who declared praise to and hope in God even when God allowed adversities one after the other (Job 13:15).

Let's Pray Together

"I also tell you this:
If two of you agree down here on earth concerning
anything you ask, my Father in heaven
will do it for you." NLT
Matthew 18:19

Gracious Lord,

Thank You for Your holy fire that consumes the dross and anything that does not please You or glorify You in my life. You want me to be pure and holy in Your sight so You commanded me to be holy for You, the Lord my God, are holy. As Jesus is the groom and I, along with other disciples, your church, the bride, You want me to be without spot or wrinkle. I submit to Your cleansing, to Your purification, to Your sanctification. I believe You will enable me to go through the process for it is Your will. I have to agree with You, abide in You, and let Your Word abide in me. Grant me the serenity that comes out of Your abiding Presence and the mind of Christ when fiery chaos come in any place I will be. I believe that the safest place is to be in the center of Your perfect will – no place I would rather be, but in that place. Whatever happens to my physical body, the truth remains that to live is Christ, to die is gain. Holy Spirit set my heart on fire to love You always Lord Jesus Amen.

Living Life in the Shadow of Death

Reflective Questions

1. What is your reaction when you hear the sound of fire alarm in a building, house, apartment, or workplace?

   _____

   _____

2. How do you understand with the description of God as "The Consuming Fire?"

   _____

   _____

3. Why do you think people panic during fire accidents? How about you?

   _____

   _____

4. Have you helped someone during or after a fire? How did you feel after doing so?

   _____

   _____

5. How does loss of things or life mean to you? What do you gain from losing money, things, person, or relationship?

   _____

   _____

"Immediately after this, Jesus made his disciples get back into the boat and cross to the other side of the lake while he sent the people home. Afterward he went up into the hills by himself to pray. Night fell while he was there alone. Meanwhile, the disciples were in trouble far away from land, for a strong wind had risen, and they were fighting heavy waves.
About three o'clock in the morning Jesus came to them, walking on the water. When the disciples saw him, they screamed in terror, thinking he was a ghost. But Jesus spoke to them at once.
'It's all right,' he said,
'I am here! Don't be afraid.'
Then Peter called to him, 'Lord, if it's really you, tell me to come to you by walking on water.'
'All right, come,'
Jesus said. So Peter went over the side of the boat and walked on the water toward Jesus. But when he looked around at the high waves, he was terrified and began to sink,
'Save me, Lord!' he shouted.
Instantly Jesus reached out his hand and grabbed him.

*'You don't have much faith,' Jesus said.
'Why did you doubt me?'*

*And when they climbed back into the boat,
the wind stopped. Then the disciples worshiped him.
'You really are the Son of God!' they exclaimed.
After they had crossed the lake,
they landed at Gennesaret.*

*The news of their arrival spread quickly
throughout the whole surrounding area,
and soon people were bringing
all their sick to be healed.
The sick begged him to let them touch
even the fringe of his robe,
and all who touched it were healed."*
Matthew 14:22-36 NLT

CHAPTER 11
THREATS ON WATERS

The Crossover

A neighborhood Bible study in Davao City, known as the biggest city, area-wise, in the Philippines, was instrumental in my knowing the God of the Bible. I was spiritually born early in 1982 during the height of the Charismatic and Pentecostal movement in the Philippines. I believe it attributed to my fast growth of faith.

We decided to go on a mission trip to a little town of Cantilan in Surigao, a province very far from Davao City where we resided. We took the opportunity to travel on a long holiday weekend. Together with my husband and I were four other couples; Maning and Mila, Bobby and Winda, Celso and Vicky, and Manny and Vicky, who agreed to join our resources for an evangelistic trip. We were like apostles of Jesus who embarked on a missionary journey outside Jerusalem and dared to tread the untrodden paths.

At about 5:00 o'clock in the morning on a fair sunny day, the ten of us left Davao City. The weather cooperated with us as we drove along the way. From Metro Davao City across the provinces of Davao del Norte and Agusan del Sur were cemented roads along generally flat terrain. It took us about seven hours of driving. When we entered the province of Surigao del Sur, northwest of Agusan del Sur, the roads were dusty and bumpy; yet still straight and flat terrain but gradually winding and ascending towards the mountainous and thickly forested area (Please see map[1] of Mindanao, Philippines showing distance from Davao City to Surigao on page 133). Passing through the rugged mountains, we crossed numerous wooden or dilapidated bridges, but passable. There were health and agriculture quarantine stations and military checkpoints. We had to get off from and back to the red jeepney (Toyota Tamaraw model). It was inconvenient, uncomfortable, and time consuming.

Threats On Waters

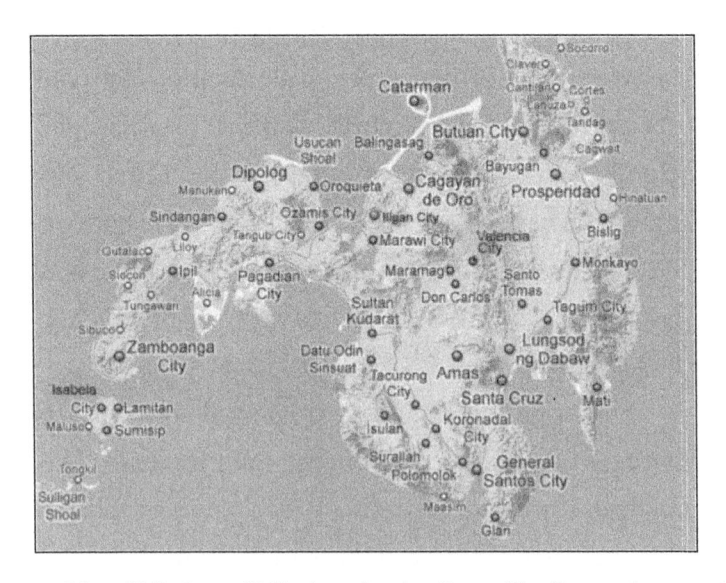

Map of Mindanao, Philippines showing Davao City (Lungsod ng Dabaw) down south and places toward the north where we travelled such as: Tagum and Monkayo of Davao del Norte province, upward to Prosperidad and Bayugan of Agusan del Sur, then farther upward through the forested area to Cantilan, Surigao del Sur.

Within the province of our destination, Surigao del Sur, but still far from the town of Cantilan, the clouds began to darken and rain started to fall. We moved on because we were in a place of no habitation. We had gone too far. Turning back to return home was not a good idea. About eight to nine hours of traveling had already passed.

Earlier during the travel, we prayed occasionally, but now we prayed continuously and fervently. We realized it was not an ordinary storm, but a typhoon. The rain was heavy with strong winds. In the Philippines, the term storm is interchangeably used to mean typhoon which is hurricane in the United States.

Then, we reached a point where we had to stop. An impassable river was before us and we couldn't cross. The torrential rains had incapacitated us from moving on with our travel. The fast flowing waters of the river created sounds and foamy waves like sea waters rushing to the shore. The waters were gushing strongly causing the wooden bridge to be under water. How could we reach the other side? What could we do in the non-stop rain and a flash flooding?

At the same instance, it would be dangerous to stay here until night time. Looking around at our location, we were reminded of the fact that we were in the midst of a jungle, in the forested hinterland, in the province where many communist rebels operate. It was getting late in the afternoon; soon, the evening's darkness will envelope our surrounding – rocky, unpaved road, undeveloped, without electricity.

The other side of the river was also uninhabited. However, more or less two hours of slow driving with the same road condition was a small town where we could spend the night. But how could we get to the other side of the river? We prayed like we never prayed before.

We were in a dilemma because all options were scary, unpredictable, or impossible: forward – by crossing the river with submerged bridge, staying on the spot – by spending the night in the river bank with unsafe surrounding, sideward – where there were no other roads, or moving back with the same route and road condition from dusk to midnight in the storm. In our land trip from the point of origin, our destination (coastal town of Cantilan) can only be reached by passing through the mountain ranges in the forested and undeveloped province of Surigao del Sur. All roads there during those years were unpaved, sand and gravel. Then, we reached the river with submerged bridge at the point in time of the typhoon.

We decided to risk the crossing. The bridge was constructed with only two long wooden beams parallel to each other with several horizontal beams across them. There were no side bars and upper parts that most bridges have. The two long beams were wide enough for a person on each beam or for the wheels of cars.

Bobby and my husband went ahead to walk on each beam to guide the jeepney which carried the rest of us. We had to confront fear with faith, and faced the danger with boldness, courage, and faith in the God we serve who empowers us with love and sound mind in times like these (2 Timothy 1:7).

In nature, anything can happen. The raindrops fell strongly to the point that the wiper blades could not clear the jeepney's windshield. The driver, Manny, had his own share of walking on waters with his red Toyota Tamaraw. The flash flood in the river could strike the legs of the men; they could slide and be swept away along with the jeep and the rest of us. All of us could be drowned. With unity in the Spirit, we took the risk to cross the river through the hazardous bridge, believing that there's nothing too difficult for God. The men before the car seemed to be walking on waters because the wooden bridge was immersed in the river. Not only did the men who walked on the wooden bridge to guide the jeep get wet. We also got wet inside the jeep, because the side windows and back were covered only by thick plastic shields, sort of an improvised tarpaulin; and the water leaked on us. I was seated at the back. I remember that when we reached the road in the storm, there were times I would held some parts of the plastic shield tightly to lessen the influx of water. (Please see the picture of a Tamaraw Toyota model[2] on page 138).

The trip was not for a pleasant vacation, but for an evangelistic outreach to the relatives of our Bible study leaders, Maning and Mila. We were compelled by the Holy Spirit in our hearts, and motivated by compassion for souls who needed God's miracle.

We faced nature's storm with prayer to the throne room of God who delights to hear the voices of His children. We moved slowly, step by step, little by little, with one focus – to trust fully in God. We combated fear because if the river had been flowing strong for a long while, it was possible that the wooden bridge became weak and our weight could break the bridge. We didn't mind the hurdle, danger, and time. With careful steps, like walking on eggs, our goal was to reach the other side.

Living Life in the Shadow of Death

The picture above shows the same model of the Toyota Tamaraw jeepney that we used for the evangelistic trip, but the color of the jeepney we used was red.

When we all landed on the other side of the river, we rejoiced and took a deep breath of relief. We raised our voices in victory saying Halleluiah! Praise God! Thank you, Jesus! We had a firsthand experience of knowing beyond any shadow of a doubt what a mighty God we served.

Our group imagined how it was with Moses and the Hebrew people who passed the Red Sea through dry land by God's miracle provision, how they rejoiced when they reach the other side and Miriam initiated the tambourine dance with other women who joined. We had our share of crossover, spiritually and physically.

Drenched, but joyful and thankful for God's help and deliverance, we continued our journey. We reached the nearby small town and there seemed to be no hotel. The wind abated and the rain subsided. Compelled by our urgent need, we stopped by a two-story house, and dared to knock and ask for help.

Lo and behold, when somebody opened the door, our Bible study leader recognized the residents. He didn't know beforehand that the tiny locality was his friends' hometown. All of us were received with kindness. Dinner was served with hot soup, for they understood that we were wet and feeling cold. We were able to refresh ourselves, change clothes, and sleep well for the night. Coincidental? No. God ordained our steps, and fit together the parts of the jigsaw puzzle.

The following morning, everyone back in the jeep, we were ready to proceed to our destination. However, another problem arose. The car wouldn't run. After several attempts and checking the engine and other parts, it still didn't start. It wouldn't move. So, we agreed to pray, believing that God could do anything. There's nothing He cannot do when His children are in urgent need. We laid hands on the jeep and prayed. We kept on praying and praying until the engine started. Another miracle of provision came. We didn't know how and we didn't know why, but it happened. We just believed God worked in ways more than we could think or imagine. Truly, our "extremes" (end of the rope) were God's opportunity to show up.

Finally, we arrived at our destination. Without further delays and not taking time to rest, we began our activities: home visitations, spread the hope in Jesus and His Word to anyone we met, home Bible studies and prayer. All these resulted in the manifestation of miracles of salvation, healing, and deliverance among many people right before our eyes. My husband and I witnessed for the first time signs and wonders happening as we laid our hands on the sick and they recovered. We heard the testimonies from the people we prayed over. We were inexperienced neophytes but full of faith in the promise of the Great Commission. When we go and proclaim the good news or the gospel to all creation (Mark 16:15), God is true to His promise – He will surely be with us always to the very end of the age (Matthew 28:20). We returned home rejoicing over the unforgettable experiences we encountered.

Immobilized

"There are green meadows and there are still waters, but I believe they are mostly to be found in places where trials most abound."[3]

Charles Spurgeon

Years passed. My family relocated to another city. Major change, and accompanying minor changes, needs a lot of adjustments. One of the other changes was my ministry activities. In the former city, I encountered only one ministry trip. This time, there were more than I planned or desired in my entire life. After settling into our new home, my ministry commitments developed from city-based to province, to area of provinces, and then to additional areas in the Visayas islands which is the middle region of the three regions in the Philippines. Travel was a necessary component of my ministry.

The Philippines is a country of approximately 7,110 islands including some islands that disappear depending on the tide. The middle region is composed of islands in between two big masses of islands, Luzon in the north and Mindanao in the South. I travelled from city to city, island to island in the middle region.

In two of those island travels, I again encountered scary situations. One was during a trip from an island province in the east side when I rode a passenger ship in going back home to the west side. I usually took the same ship in my return trip. We were more than halfway when the engine stopped.

From my cot I had a view of the smoke coming out of the space where the engine was. I looked outside. There was no island in the vicinity, nor was any land visible from afar. I saw only sea waters all around. I didn't know how to swim, I had never learned. Hopefully, the boat would not sink, no shark would smell flesh, and there would be no sudden change of weather.

It was beautiful that day. The blue sky was decorated with cumulus clouds like huge bunches of cotton candy. The sea was calm and the aquamarine waves, capped with silver glitters, glinted in the sunshine. What a lovely sight, except that we were stranded in salty waters.

I shuddered at the thought of drowning, even though I saw where the lifejackets were situated. Quickly, I rejected that appalling thought. I read my Bible and prayed. I remembered Apostle Paul's shipwreck during his missionary travels and he overcame the dangers. How about me in this situation? I just came from a speaking commitment, building up the faith of women. It would be shame on me if I couldn't encourage myself in the Lord.

One of the crew walked near where I was standing. I took the chance to open a conversation with him that led to sharing encouraging scriptures in the hearing range of the other passengers. Whatever might happen, at least I had spoken about hoping and trusting in the Lord. I thanked God there was no abrupt commotion among the passengers that could have caused the boat to tilt and capsize.

I went back to my cot and prayed. I prayed for the captain and the crew, prayed for the ship itself especially the engine, prayed for the passengers, prayed for my family back home, and more as the Holy Spirit led me.

The passengers were alert, watchful, and waiting for updated announcements. We heard from the crew that a rescue message was sent. Another ship would come and tow our ship to our destination. In a way, the news alleviated the anxiety of the passengers. Minutes passed... and more minutes... and an hour... and past an hour. There was still no sign of an approaching rescue ship. After much waiting – patiently waiting – we heard the sound of the engine. "It's working – amazing!" I exclaimed. I didn't want to ask what happened. I just wanted to praise my wonderful God. He'll make a way when hope and possibility are lost.

In our journey in life we can be immobilized, whether in a valley, on a mountaintop, or in the midst of the sea such as our situation. We cannot move backward, sideward, or forward. The only way we can move is upward. Lift our voices, audible or inaudible to the heavens, to the Almighty God who delivers, who rescues, who is always waiting and eager to hear from us, to bless us in any way because He is the God of blessing. He never wills that we suffer. He'll make possible what is impossible for us. In our immobility we can mobilize our own faculties of mind, heart, and body to align with God. With ourselves or with others, we can activate prayers. The devil wants to immobilize us, but God frees us and causes us to triumph. We cannot move, but God moves. Then we move forward with Him, with renewed assurance and joy.

Storm at Sea

"Then Jesus got into the boat and started across the lake with his disciples. Suddenly, a terrible storm came up, with waves breaking into the boat.
But Jesus was sleeping.
The disciples went to him and woke him up, shouting, 'Lord, save us! We're going to drown!'
And Jesus answered,
'Why are you afraid? You have so little faith!'
Then he stood up and rebuked the wind and waves, and suddenly all was calm. The disciples
just sat there in awe.
'Who is this? They asked themselves.
'Even the wind and waves obey him!'"
Matthew 8:23-27 NLT

I passed the crossover miracle in the 1980s and another one in the 1990s when another storm blast occurred. Again, I was in another island trip. This time, I was not alone. My aged mother was with me. She loved to travel, unlike me. What gave me boldness, courage, and joy in travels was simply the loving surrender to my Lord Jesus who opened my spirit to genuine peace in life, living for Jesus more than for myself. Life became meaningful. His truth became worth living far more than worldly aspirations measured in position, possession, wealth, and popularity. I feel contented and fulfilled in obeying and pleasing Him. It included breaking the borders of my comfort zones; one was my personal preference to stay at home, always close to my family.

Just like the previous danger mentioned, this sea peril occurred on our travel back home. In the middle of our trip, a stormy wind blew intensely and waves rocked the ship from both sides. The passengers hurriedly pulled down the tarpaulin to cover us. The strong rain that poured diagonally hit the side where we were. My mother and I transferred our few belongings as we quickly moved to the middle part of the ship. Traveling light was such an advantage in that situation. Unlike us, those in the cabins were protected from the rain. They were few, the rest of us were many.

Prayer is my lifestyle, so I am more likely to practice it in times like this. My mother and I joined together in prayer. She had hypertension; hence, I persisted in my plea for God's help. I remembered the story of Jesus commanding the wind and the sea and they obeyed Jesus' words. My heart leaped. My faith escalated. Declaring the authority of the name of Jesus that is above every name, mightier than the mightiest storm; I prayed commanding the wind and the rain to stop and the waves to keep calm. We continually prayed while sitting in the lower part of a two-story bunk bed. The ship tossed to and fro. Though my pulse raced, my heart was steadfast trusting in the Lord who promised present help in times of trouble. He is always in control. "Oh God, my heavenly Father, please rescue us, save us. Please hear our prayers and stop the storm."

The boisterous sounds of the wind and rain and the splashing waves were frightening. The battle with nature was advancing again; seething... ranting... lashing against our petite and frail physique. I covered my mom and myself with blankets because the rain hit us whenever the wind struck. We were warned not to move to the other side as it could have caused the three-level ship to capsize. So, we stayed where we were.

My mom and I are small women, but the two of us – together – can agree on anything on earth in Jesus' name and it will be done (Matthew 18:19-20). We kept on praying. We were so focused on praying that we didn't notice when the storm stopped. After a long while we opened our eyes, and there was no more heavy rain, no more monster wind, no more raving waves. Jesus saves yesterday, today, and always.

Let's Pray Together

*"I also tell you this:
If two of you agree down here on earth concerning
anything you ask, my Father in heaven
will do it for you."* NLT
Matthew 18:19

*Gracious Lord,
Thank You for Your Hand of protection over my life.
You shield me from harm and danger, seen and unseen.
I do not know what the day will bring, but You, Oh
God, with unlimited knowledge, know full well. You
are already ahead of me and have taken control of
whatever impending catastrophe anywhere I would
be. My finite mind can't comprehend, but I believe You,
I put my trust in You. You are truly omniscient, omnipotent, and omnipresent. However deep or wide the sea
and river, You can reach me. Nothing is beyond Your
power to rescue me. You didn't create me to live on
waters, may it be physical or waters of adversity, but
to journey along for a time with purpose. With Your
sufficient grace, the slam of the waves, the deafening
howling of the wind, and the terrifying lightning and
thunder are all bearable because You are with me.*

That is all that matters. They cannot shake me; they cannot harm me for You surround me with Your holy, mighty Presence. The sky, land, and waters will listen and stop at Your command. All creation bows down before You. Through stormy seas or peaceful waters, cause me to be steadfast, always abounding in doing what You purposed me to live in every season of my life. With You and through You, I can do all things for You strengthen me. In Your name Jesus I pray, Amen.

Reflective Questions

1. Have you experienced crossing a river or sailing from island to island? What thoughts came to your mind as you were on the trip?

   _____

   _____

   _____

2. How do you relate with transitions in life?

   _____

   _____

3. How do you feel being stranded during one of your trips? It maybe engine trouble, accident, or cancellation of flights or for whatever reason.

   _____

   _____

4. How did such experiences shape your knowledge of God?

   _____

   _____

CHAPTER 12
BATTLE IN THE WOMB

*"Then the Lord your God will make you most
prosperous in all the work of your hands and in
the fruit of your womb…
See, I set before you today life and prosperity,
death and destruction…
This day I call heaven and earth as witnesses
against you that I have set before you life and
death, blessings and curses.
Now choose life, so that you and your children
may live and that you may love the Lord your
God, listen to his voice, and hold fast to him.
For the Lord is your life…"* (NIV)
Deuteronomy 30:9, 15, 19-20

How would you feel if you learned that you could have died before you were born, not because of an accident or calamity, but because of human plan or decision? You would feel unwelcomed, rejected, unloved. Those were my feelings. My mind kept forming questions: Why? What possible reason could cause that kind of decision? A baby is supposed to be a fruit of love between a man and a woman.

In those younger years as a busy working mother of three, intimate conversations with my mother were very seldom. I really had to purposely make time for it. One day, my mother who was living with me, revealed something. *"I tried different ways to end my pregnancy, but you came out alive any way."* Silence filled the air.

I didn't know how to respond. I was staring straight ahead of me. This was unimaginable – I could have been a victim of willful abortion. *How about me as a mother?* Every baby I carried in my womb was cherished; each one was special. I took care of myself and each one of them from the time life started in my womb. My unspoken question was, *"But me, why?"* Only the two of us were at home, in the bedroom during that private encounter. It was so quiet . . . I could hear my heartbeat. The stillness of the moment dragged. Then... a sound came.

My mother broke the silence. She explained that it happened because my father and she were not wed in church. What a shallow, dismal reason! How does religious culture intensely shape and deeply influence the mindset of people? My mother's perspective was sharply twisted. How could she allow the living, breathing being inside of her to suffer the consequences of her frustration? What crime did the unborn commit to endure agony in confinement and ultimately die? Helpless and defenseless, the unborn can't do anything to avert such an outcome, and can't understand why he/she is there. Why should a delicate and alive human being not be granted the right, will, and chance to live? *It could have been me.* My innermost being shouted, *this is unfair.*

Life is life, it is precious, and it is to be handled with extra tender loving care. However, the new person in me abides in Christ who reminds us every now and then, "forgive them for they know not what they do" Luke 23:34 (KJV). I must do likewise. Although I cannot accept her reason as justifiable, I have to honor and respect my mother in obedience to Christ and His Word. I have to understand that my mother lived in a time and locale when and where a church wedding was a ticket to acceptance among married women in the community. A civil wedding didn't satisfy the parameters of that religious culture, downplaying the legality thereof.

Shame became a forceful justification to choose death. Poor Mama! She was a victim of the socio-psychological religious culture of her world then and she didn't know Christ personally, yet.

A raging battle between life and death had begun. I was attacked in my mother's womb, already sentenced to die in the earliest moment of life. The turmoil I went through in those nine long months of being shaped in obscurity and anonymity was surrounded by sorts of toxins, hurts, and pains. My mother confessed that she would drink something (I don't remember what specific drink it was) that could abort me, scrub the floor, and do other things she could think of. I could just imagine how a mighty tiny warrior I was, fighting for life against the odds. It was worth it all. Death did not come at my birth. Life came out victorious. I was born alive and well, without complication, and without sickness. I fought a good fight from the beginning and survived under the mighty hand of the One who gave me breath and life. My Maker had wired in me the make-up of a tenacious, resolute fighter for life. Praise God, He intervened. Thank you Lord, I owe it all to you.

As God is the source of life, Satan is the author of death. Whatever is of God, Satan opposes. So, every life that begins is welcomed by death to thwart God's purpose and blessing. God commanded Adam and Eve to multiply, but Eve's disobedience cursed her with intense pain and suffering in childbearing (Gen. 3:16a). Have you not wondered why there is death in childbirth either to the infant or to the mother? I remember my older sister, Beatriz, who died immediately after giving birth to her one and only child. The sadder thought is that there are deaths prior to birth, not by accident, but by the willful decision of mothers.

The deception of the devil to Eve continues and could be passed from generation to generation until today. The evil one steals, kills, and destroys. He steals the joy of motherhood with disappointment, frustration, and bitterness and dumps all the blame on the poor innocent creature inside of her. Woman believes the lie that the solution is to exterminate the unborn. Children are gifts and a heritage from God. Some mothers reject the gift and believe they have control over the life they don't own.

Without the grace of God, I could have hated my mother. The feelings of an unwanted child can only be healed by the love of God in Christ.

For those who survive birth, death comes in other forms such as sickness or accidents. The author of death attacks like a roaring lion to find every opportunity to annihilate life sooner than the gospel could come to the person and have a chance to repent and receive Christ and eternal life. The devil knows that man is destined to die only once, then comes judgment (Hebrews 9:27). The devil cannot match the extravagant love, grace, and mercy of God who does not will that anyone be destroyed but that everyone will repent and live a transformed life throughout eternity (2 Peter 3:9). God still makes a way for everyone, giving chances after chances even until man's last breath. The devil relentlessly deceives and attacks people. He pursues and persists to destroy, not only things and property, but relationships as well (including between mothers and daughters), causing biting of one another until everyone is consumed (Gal. 5:15). Then the devil enjoys raucous laughter.

Fights, whether small-scale or large-scale, among individuals, groups, families – between or among parents and children, tribes, and nations, are basically the same. Regardless of magnitude, the bottom line is division and destruction. Knowing the schemes, it is best not to allow the enemy to cripple our present and future but rather trust in the One who gave life and promised to make it abundant and free with loving relationships.

Let's Pray Together

*"I also tell you this:
If two of you agree down here on earth concerning
anything you ask, my Father in heaven
will do it for you."* NLT
Matthew 18:19

Gracious Lord,
Thank You for breathing Your breath of life into my unformed body. You made it grow strong to full development and become healthy at birth. I was helpless in the womb yet already exposed and facing exterminators. But Your gentle care is more than enough. No heartless, ruthless intruder of destruction and death can overpower Your amazing love and good plan. I agree to Your assurance that no weapon formed against me shall prosper. You are the omnipotent One; no other power can withstand You. My life is safe in Your Hands. I can't thank You enough for this initial stage of my life in the womb where You have prepared me to face the harsh realities outside. Then and there at the beginning You have taught my inner being to fight for good against evil. You caused me to be a victor not a victim, a winner not a whiner, a

conqueror, not a defeatist. You pushed me out into the world where You want me to fulfill Your purpose. I am humbled with this truth. Your full knowledge is outstanding and astounding; I am awed. Lord, forbid that I go astray from this truth. On bended knees and heart I implore Your Holy Spirit, please empower me to live according to Your plan and purpose. Help me Lord Jesus I pray, Amen.

Reflective Questions

1. How do you feel whenever your birthday draws near? What makes you feel happy? Why? What makes you feel sad? Why?

   _____

   _____

   _____

2. Were you a healthy baby when you were born? How did it affect your growing years and adulthood, in your attitude, in your relationships, in your performance, etc.?

   _____

   _____

   _____

3. How was your concept and belief in God shaped by your experience at birth and growing years?

   _____

   _____

   _____

   _____

PART V

THE RESTORATION - TOWARDS ABUNDANT LIFE!

CHAPTER 13
REST TO REFRESH

—⚜—

"And I say, 'Oh, that I had wings like a dove!
I would fly away and be at rest;
Yes, I would wander far away;
I would lodge in the wilderness;
I would hurry to find a shelter
From the raging wind and tempest.'"
Psalm 55:6-8 ESV

"Come to me, all who labor and are heavy laden,
and I will give you rest.
Take my yoke upon you, and learn from me,
for I am gentle and lowly in heart,
and you will find rest for your souls.
For my yoke is easy, and my burden is light."
Matthew 11:28-30 ESV

When we visit the gravesite of a family member, relative, or friend, we read the initials R.I.P. engraved on the stone markers. In walking around a cemetery, we read the same initials. They have long been associated with the dead. We console ourselves with the thought that they are in a better place. They are done with life's struggles and we are still here, striving, struggling, and working hard. This common belief has obscured the truth that rest is also for the living. Peace is for the living too. We often hear "God bless you" or "peace be with you." Why can't we say "rest in peace," or "rest in His peace," or "rest be with you" to someone? Jesus Christ comforted His disciples,

"Peace I leave with you; my peace I give to you; not as the world gives do I give to you. Do not let your heart be troubled, nor let it be fearful" (John 14:27 NASB).

Paul encouraged the troubled disciples to rest with them (2 Thessalonians 1:7). When we believe God's assurance, we have peace. When we don't believe, we have no rest (Hebrews 3:18-19).

From the time we are birthed from our mother's womb, we are laid down to rest by a midwife, by a nurse, or by our own mother. We are cared for and helped. Otherwise, our fragile human frame couldn't sustain the sudden change from the peace within the womb into the strange atmosphere outside. By some means, rest was made available. It may not be by the caring arms of a medical team, but it can be in unusual ways outside somewhere as God ordains and orchestrates for a life to be at rest and be preserved. Sometimes the sovereign will and ways of God are incomprehensible to our limited understanding. We are awed when we read, hear, or watch news of babies recovered or rescued from places we never thought they could survive. I, too, rested after I was launched out into the world after fighting all odds inside my mother's womb.

This availability of rest comes as we grow into childhood, to adolescence, to adulthood, and to maturing years. Toddlers learn to walk and run, then rest and try again. Children seem to play indefatigably, but they do rest. Adults may be workaholics, but they find time to rest, or else reap the consequence detrimental to their health and safety. Seniors work too, whether in a job or not, and continue to participate in productive activities. Life is tough and tiresome, but there are spans of time in between for rest.

As work is part of life, rest is also part of it – of living life. Yes, we toil, but our life is not all toil. Every activity under the sun is a partnership between work and rest. It is in resting that we are refreshed and restored to vitality and strength. Now and then, we need to make time to rest.

This is ordained by God. He rested on the seventh day after creation. He modeled rest for us because He knows our limits. When we don't heed the warning signs, our body falls into menacing decline and we suffer. Sometimes, we become deaf and blind to warning signs. Our focus becomes myopic with the single thought and deceptive expediency that hard work, perseverance, and endurance will guarantee success; forgetting we are humans and not robots or machines. We need to avoid extremes and live a balanced life. Paul counseled the disciples to be restrained, or considerate in conducting their lives (Philippians 4:5).

Rest does not mean doing nothing. We still breathe, move, and have our being. Our hearts are still pumping, our minds are still thinking, and we are still breathing. We rest while we are still alive. Don't you? Of course, I do too.

After awakening from a coma, I rested. Hours became days, days became weeks, and weeks became months. I never knew rest in the real sense of the word until I experienced that prolonged season. Did I like it? No. That was the last thing I wanted to do. My human nature shouted action, but at that time, my spirit whispered rest. Following my personal tendencies and preferences, I would have obstructed my body's defense mechanism and weakened my immune system. I needed to cooperate with God's provision for natural healing to take place and work its best for my good. Instead, in the stillness of rest, I yielded to God's mighty work to complete His miracle healing in the restorative process of my body, in the efficacious resurrection power of Christ's divine healing. I want none of me and more of Him. All I want for my life is to abide in Him. In the stillness of rest, I declared death to self-effort, death to preferential rights, death to "I deserve" attitude. I leaned on His embrace and abandoned myself to His will, caved in to His ways, and adhered to His time. In that season of rest, I chose to live His life, on His terms, in His purpose.

After the horrifying fire tragedy (refers to chapter 10), I rested. The blessing of rest came with the resumption of family togetherness. Family is the most precious gem I cherish, and I love them more than anything in the world next to God and the Lord Jesus Christ. Their voices in conversation, the grins and smiles on their faces, their hands helping with household chores; every sight and sound, anything that would authenticate their presence is joy, peace, and contentment for me. I returned home with thanks to God for preserving my life, so I can continue to be with my children in their growing years. The unpredictability of the future demands that I enjoy my time with my family while I'm alive and well. Like a bird, plant, tree, or any other living creature on earth, I am here today and gone tomorrow. Hence, like savoring a meal to the last bite, every second of every minute spent with my family is to be relished. I reveled in every bit of their presence at that time of rest back home.

After each threatening journey on the waters, I rested. The journeys on seas and crossing a river threatened us with deadly and impending perils. But the ever-present God is always available, a present help in time of trouble (Psalm 46:1), and provides a time, a place, a way to rest after each ordeal such as: a house to stay in the night after a risky river crossing, a safe arrival at our destination after a tempestuous storm, and after a possible shipwreck due to engine fire in another trip. God contrived a way for me to ease my mind, to calm my pounding heart, and to abate my tensions. The ordeals did not stop me from doing what He called me to do and from going where He wanted me to go. I rested when I had to, but I didn't quit, and still won't.

After my battle for life before, during, and after birth, I rested. I have always believed that I was cared for from the time I was born and proper rest was afforded to me. As far as memory serves, I did not get sick in my childhood and growing years. My father cared for me all those years, loved me, protected me, and dreamed for my future. All through those years of growing and maturing, rest was always part of every endeavor and pursuit.

The loud cry at birth is temporary and is quieted by God's providence that is permanent and constant. His rest makes a baby slumber with or without a lullaby.

Unlike all the preceding scenarios where I rested by force of circumstances, now I resolve to rest every now and then. It seems fit and necessary to gather strength and move into the destiny that God has purposed for me to be, has ordained for me to do, and accomplish as long as I live on this planet earth until

I stand before Him face to face in all of His glory. Then will I hear His invitation to share and celebrate His joy with Him (Matthew 25:21). He rewards our faithfulness, though He is more faithful than we could ever be. Even our faithfulness is made possible by His enablement and provision through various ways of rest appropriate for our specific time of need.

Elijah, one of the major prophets in the Old Testament, received provision for food and rest to accomplish his assignment. After prophesying to King Ahab that there would be no rain in Israel for the succeeding years, God instructed him to go to a place near the brook of Cherith so he could drink from the brook. Furthermore, He commanded the ravens to bring Elijah food while He rested for a while. Elijah took time and effort with courage and boldness to travel for a challenging mission – talked to the highest authority in the land and declared something negative. Is it not stressful? Sure enough! It could be that Elijah fought an inner battle not to succumb to political expediency, but to obey the call of God though it may have been inconvenient and dangerous. He chose to please God and not man, though the king was the most powerful person in the country. It could be nerve-wrenching and gut-exhausting to carry out God's command.

Thereafter, he needed to calm himself in a place for a time of respite. That rest was enough for him to gather a stockpile of courage for the next assignments. He worked a miracle in Zarepath according to God's guidance and instruction and performed another stupendous miracle at Mount Carmel. Amazing God! Those miraculous feats gained glory to God but consequently did not exempt Elijah from the attacks of the devil and human cohorts. He became the target of the vicious slander of Jezebel, King Ahab's wife. She vowed to avenge for the death of her Baal prophets by pursuing Elijah to death.

Frustration, depression, and fear overwhelmed the prophet. Instead of confronting the harassment of the enemy, he wanted to die. He was echoing the enemy's scheme to end his ministry and life. His gigantic faith during the miracles soon dwarfed into void. In a short time, he was engulfed with tremendous fright and became frozen-still. Yet, God showed His loving mercy and care for His servant and prophet. He sent an angel to Elijah who was tired and weary from running for his life. Finding Elijah in his solitude, the angel woke him and gave him food. Then he slept again. He lost the zeal to do anything for God and zest for life. The food and rest that were provided for Elijah were sufficient to refresh and revive him; not for nothing or to do nothing, but to do something. He was due for a long haul, a long and great travel for him. Rest was vital for him to continue the course set for him.

As a new Christian in the early 1980s one of the songs taught to our Bible study group was inspired from 1 Corinthians 9:24-25. We were encouraged to continually run the race in our earthly journey and depend on God's enabling power for victory. We don't demand from God what is to be done with our life in any season or location. The final rest may be near or far, but the truth remains that in every season of rest in this evanescent world, there is renewal and restoration. We rest, if and when we need to, but we don't stop unless God's signal says so.

Rest is God's ordained component of life – of **living life**.

Let's Pray Together

*"I also tell you this:
If two of you agree down here on earth concerning
anything you ask, my Father in heaven
will do it for you."* NLT
Matthew 18:19

Gracious Lord,
Here I am, wanting to rest in Your loving arms. After all the vicissitudes and turmoil of life, I run to You. I need You, I want You. Keep me in Your solid ground and gain the strength I need to move on to the next hurdle, next step, and next level for the best is yet to come. Thank You for these times of rest so that I can pause, ponder, and perceive new revelation, or so that I can halt in Your interruption and obey You, or so that I can be filled with awe and interjection with Your amazing shielding and interventions in the battlefield. Thank You for helping me fight the good fight of faith, letting me rest so I won't be tired and weary because of Your awesome Presence that never leaves, but keeps on embracing me, whether at rest or on the go. Yes Lord, I won't quit because the battle is already won by You at the cross. I shout my voice

in praise to You for the victory is mine through Your sacrificial death. I declare I am restful because You are in control of everything in my life. I will rest in the bounties of Your praise, prayer, and Presence in Jesus' name, Amen.

Reflective Questions

1. What is the first thing that comes to your mind when you hear the word "rest"?

   _____

   _____

   _____

2. Do you wrestle against work or rest? Why? How?

   _____

   _____

   _____

3. How do you balance yourself between work and rest?

   _____

   _____

   _____

4. How do you take care of your body from "workhaholism" or stress?

   _____

   _____

   _____

5. How did you abound after you spend a time of rest?

_____

_____

_____

_____

CHAPTER 14

REBOUND TO ABOUND

―❦―

"O storm-battered city, troubled and desolate! I will rebuild you on a foundation of sapphires and make the walls of your houses from precious jewels."
Isaiah 54:11 NLT

Have you ever experienced a car collision? I have. Twice, I was a passenger with my husband driving when our car was involved in an accident. The first was in January 2007 when we were transferring from my church assignment in Long Beach, CA to my new church assignment in Pomona, CA. The uncertainty and mixed emotions of excitement and anxiety that accompany new beginnings intensified our reactions to a car accident on the first day of the first month of the year of our new church life.

While we were eastbound along Freeway 105, our car was impacted by a sudden strong bump with accompanying loud sound. I was shocked. The vehement force jerked our bodies forward. We could have been seriously injured or killed. After the Suburban SUV smacked and smashed our red Montero, it propelled swiftly through our right side turning left and almost turned turtle in front close to us. Then it immediately bounced back upright and drove away from us fast and furious! We didn't notice there were highway patrolmen in a car behind us who saw the accident and quickly chased the escaping runaway driver. The driver must have been so frantic that he drove horizontally crossing through the four lanes toward the exit. The accident happened so suddenly and unexpectedly that we paused, stunned, and didn't know what to do. We were still feeling groggy when a highway patrol officer on a motorcycle approached us. He asked questions, verified the physical impact on us, and advised us what to do next. He seemed concerned what could have had happened to us. Thank God for the seat belts; the benefit of obeying the rules profits much.

The second collision occurred two years later. Our car's rear end was banged again. It was on a Friday evening on our way after a Bible study. The first accident had caused severe damage to the body; the second accident likewise severely damaged our car, though unlike the way it was with the first. However, it created a sting of phobia in me.

The truth hit me that the enemy of our soul is a destruction-hunter, people-slaying, and venomous killer who is continually at work against all people – the apple of God's eyes. How much more he does to believers and minister servants of the Lord. He constantly devises all means to exterminate anyone at a moment before God's appointed time or before God's plan and purpose be fulfilled in our lives.

However, this is only one side of the truth. The other side is that Jesus has already come into my heart and life. I no longer live my own life. Instead I live His life, and enjoy His eternal life, that I received by faith (John 3:16, Galatians 2:20, 1 John 5:12). I should not entertain any cloud of condemnation because I already have passed from death – with varied colors, attacks, and deceptions – to life that began when I received Jesus Christ as my personal Savior and Lord (John 5:24).

The eternal life God offers is not waiting beyond the blue skies but it begins right at the moment; at the very minute we decide to choose Jesus and not the devil, the world, and/or the big self in us as the Lord of our lives. It continues until we meet Him in the clouds (1 Thessalonians 4:17) and be with Him forever. He promised abundant life versus destruction and death from the enemy of our soul. So we live life – we are living life – even in the midst of the attacks of the devil in various forms and times. Jesus is the Good Shepherd who assures us that even when we walk in paths where the shadow of death is pursuing to crush us, we should not be afraid or troubled, because His rod will drive away the enemy and his cohorts; His staff will rescue us, lift us up, and comfort us with His restorative healing (Psalm 23:4). What the devil means for bad or harm, God can and will reverse and thwart the enemy's scheme with His shield of protection. Preservation of my husband and me in those two car collisions were examples of His protection. Sound ominous? Maybe it was, maybe not. Life can be uncertain and portentous with attacks from the enemy.

Our car was repaired and restored to a running condition. After complying with chiropractic schedules, we observed improvement with our bodies and well being. What a relief to recover from trauma and phobia after each of the two accidents. After slowing down for a while, we were ready to flex our muscles and continue to do the things we needed to do. In the process, however, we had to subjugate ourselves to humbling situations that did not only bolster our faith, but exposed us to new ways of God's providential care. One example was the provision of a temporary abode after the first accident and the offering of a car for use while our car was on repair through Pastor Boyet Jose and the kindness of other staff at Charisma Life. We were also thankful for the supportive care of the lead pastor, Reverend Dr. Fred Mendoza.

Whatever collision with death or shades of death we encounter, the truth remains that we have God, not just any god or similarity thereof, but the God of Creation and Restoration. His sundry, great ways are beyond what our minds can conceive.

We abound with flamboyant thanks and praise after perils and safe destination. We abound in brushing aside negative thoughts and feelings of self pity, desperation, grief, doubt, worry, fear, and anything that would hinder us to live by faith with inner strength.

As with my coma tragedy, I rebounded as I recovered my health in a short period of two months and abounded in being productive again with the continuation of my weekly ministry in the third month. Though I have not yet regained full strength in the first month; nevertheless, it has improved slowly month after month. In less than a month, on February 2010, I was able to preach again. I rested after lunch till the end of day. It seemed my strength was enough only to preach that morning. It was followed by another preaching schedule the succeeding month, March 2010. On this month, not only did I preach once, but twice on the same Sunday. The opportunity was accompanied with a schedule for a mid-week service. In the third month, April of 2010, my Bible study was resumed and another Bible study was added. Is this not amazing? What was happening to me after recovery was completely opposite the doctor's prognosis when I was rushed to the ICU. Instead of becoming vegetated as a common result of hyponatremia, I have been alive and well, healthy and serving my God in the ministry He had called me.

Not only did I abound physically and spiritually but also cognitively. In the following year, I ventured into adult career education. I wanted to augment my elementary knowledge and skills in computer with the lowest cost possible. I found a class at a nearby location. I enrolled, finished, and graduated from a short course in Office Assistance Program at the Metropolitan Skills Center. Again, the favor of God showed up. I was able to finish the program in a short period of time; hence, I was included with the last batch of graduates before the school closed. Huge thanks to my prayer answering God!

Through this school I came to know about job openings. I came across something that I was interested in, but an exam was required. I have not taken such a competitive test for a very long time. Now I will try to do it at my age and in the U.S.? *Hello! Are you crazy?* I decided to take a chance, anyway. There's no harm in trying, as many people would say. My trying paid off. After several months of waiting, I received the result that I passed! Endless "thank you" swarmed my prayers. Several months passed and I did not receive interview calls. A few months before the one year expiration, a few calls came, but thereafter, I heard nothing definite. *Whether I land a job or not, it's fine*. I considered it a success in the sense that with my age and recent health battle, I passed the hurdles of schooling, took a countywide exam, and passed. Come to think of it, there were more than

4,000 examinees and most were younger or much younger than me.

There's more to God's work of restoration in my brain. Before the coma hit me in that foreboding day of January 28, 2010, I was enrolled in distance education in a graduate study course in "Poetry and Proverb: The Psalms and Wisdom Literature." For a certain period of time, I had to submit the required papers, assignments, or writings for every part of the subject. All these were stopped, as if my world ended at that time. After I recovered my health to the point that I could do computer tasks at home, I informed my professor and the university, Global University Graduate School, about my situation and requested an extension of deadline for my submission of requirements. My request was granted. I finished the course with outstanding grades and received encouraging commendation from my professor, Leland Ryken, with each assignment I submitted.

This sequence of events proved that God is faithful and true to His promises time and time again. He performed His word for me during my recovery stage, *"you anoint my head with oil, my cup overflows"* (Psalm 23:5b ESV). He is still the God of restoration and is powerful to cause a renewal of what's lost or destroyed. In Him I am satisfied, I am contented, and I am fulfilled.

We are created to be productive and fruitful – this is part of the image and likeness of God that we were made of. We are a reflection of the Maker. God will equip and enable us to be and to do according to His plan and purpose. As God is always at work, so are we; we are meant to work, and accomplish much as long as we live. We live according to the number of days He desires and has destined. Until then, we continue to breathe, and move, and toil, and walk in the works of God that He places in our hearts, or fulfill what we are wired, and destined to be and to do. We continue to aspire for what He continues to inspire in us.

We rebound and abound when the enemy knocks us down, because the Spirit of God in us is greater than the evil spirit in the world (1 John 4:4). We know beyond any shadow of a doubt, and believe in our heart, that we belong to God as His children, because Jesus Christ bought us with the price of His blood at the cross. We rebound and abound because Jesus is at the right hand of the Father continually interceding for us (Hebrews 7:25), and the saints who have left before us are cheering for us. No matter how many times the world and the devil reject us through people, or stab us through sickness, or destroy us through dangers of any sorts, we rise as accepted beloved children in the caring arms of our heavenly Father. He lifts us up above the waters and above the darkening clouds; confirming His untiring affirmation of love, care, and help.

We live to abound, rebound if needed, and abound again because abundance is what man was originally created for and destined to be. Let us remember that when God made Adam and Eve in the beginning of time, He commanded them to increase and to multiply. It was God's blessing for them to experience abundance, not only in the reproduction of their kind, but in fruitfulness and in taking charge of the things around them (Gen. 1:28). He gave the same command to the sea creatures (Gen. 1:20-22) and to the creatures on the land (Gen. 1:24-25). In other words, productivity and prosperity are God's will and design for all living creatures. The enemy roars in envy towards man, accusing and cursing man, but God is the God of blessing. He destined man for success and prosperity. The devil devised death for man but God designed man for abundant life here and for all eternity. Therefore, we don't dismay for we live not to fear the unknown, but to believe and wait for the unraveling and unfolding of the good things in store for us.

Let's Pray Together

*"I also tell you this:
If two of you agree down here on earth concerning
anything you ask, my Father in heaven
will do it for you."* NLT
Matthew 18:19

Gracious Lord,
Thank You for Your restoring power. You revive my soul in the quietness of Your Presence. You gather the pieces of my bruised, fragmented life then connect and weave them into a beautiful tapestry; made whole, useful, and fruitful again. Thank You for Your loving kindness par excellence, incomparable by human standards. Thank You for the humbling situations for it was there that You pick me up and showed me Your faithfulness, and the reality of who You are, and what You can do in my life. Truly, Oh Lord, the truth of who You are is mind boggling, but through the dying, near death, or life threatening experiences, or whatever difficult situation that threatens my faith in You, You show up – the great I AM, the resurrection and the life, the God of restoration. Help my focus settled in You, for without You I can do nothing. In Your

mighty name Jesus and the power of Your precious blood, I cancel the assignment of the enemy to destroy me in any way, I cancel every curse or negative word spoken against me, I cancel every word planned or spoken to insult me, mock me, despise me or assassinate my character to bring me down or destroy the work of God in my life. Bless the work of my hands that it may result to success and prosperity. Bless the gifts that You gave from the time You birthed me and developed in my growing years to adulthood. Anoint them to be useful in Your Kingdom to proclaim and introduce who You are, so that others may be blessed too. Lead me to where and how those gifts will fit me in endeavors You already prepared for me and will lead me there. I declare I am not a misfit; You will help me find my fit, and be productive and fruitful. Huge thanks for Your promise in 3 John 2, "Beloved, I wish above all things that thou mayeth prosper and be in health, even as thy soul prospereth" (KJV). Please let me abound and flourish that You may be glorified in my life. This I pray in Jesus' name, Amen.

Reflective Questions

1. How do you feel when your favorite athlete hits a successful rebound in a sports arena?

   _____

   _____

   _____

2. How did you recover from failures, mistakes, health problem, loss of finances, property, or any material things?

   _____

   _____

   _____

3. Can you identify people, institution, family, organization, things that help you on the road to recovery?

   _____

   _____

   _____

4. Why do you think it is difficult to rebound?

   _____

   _____

5. How did the scripture help you in times of difficulty and in times of rebound? In what ways did you abound?

___
___
___
___

CHAPTER 15
EXTEND TO EXPAND

"Enlarge the place of your tent, and the curtains of your habitations be stretched out; do not hold back; lengthen your cords and strengthen your stakes. For you will spread abroad to the right and to the left, and your offspring will possess the nations and will people the desolate cities." ESV
Isaiah 54:2-3

"Jabez was more honorable than his brothers; and his mother called his name Jabez, saying, 'Because I bore him in pain.' Jabez called upon the God of Israel, saying, 'Oh that you would bless me and enlarge my border, and that your hand might be with me, and that you would keep me from harm so that it might not bring me pain!' And God granted what he asked." ESV
1 Chronicles 4:9-10

Many people would love to hear words like "long" or "satisfying" or "prosperous" applied to their life. Almost all, if not all, hope for long life. As to how long they want, that changes and increases each time they approach the previously desired age. This notion is a reflection of man's desire for perpetuation of life. This desire stems from two phenomena: 1) the fear of the unknown or the hidden, lurking fear of death due to uncertainty of its consequence, 2) the immortalization of the known or the unexpressed longing to stay on earth forever. This is surprisingly normal despite the fact that we know many people who have passed away.

Anti-aging products for beauty, health, and nutrition flood the stores and dominate commercials and advertisements. Commerce and industry unmask this reality such as the retirement age in employment or in insurance products that slowly keep adding years.

God created man in His image and likeness. Part of God's likeness in man is eternal life. As a result of sin, man was separated from God and life was shortened. Adam and Eve enjoyed the privilege, authority, and prosperity in the garden until the day they succumbed to the lies of the serpent. Man was endowed with an innate consciousness of eternity, but that eternity is not in isolation from God, but rather exemplified in fellowship with Him. Since the connectivity was lost, what remained in man is the longing, the yearning, or the craving of that which was stolen by the devil with cunning device.

The tragedy of man's fall is aggravated by the pervasive pursuit of death. Death does not come at man's last breath. It comes near us anytime and in any way possible. In fact, it continually approaches and then retreats, in a never ending cycle. The attack-retreat fashion marches on with monster eyes on the lookout, creeping in, and seizing every opportunity to thwart God's move in someone's life. The angel of death poses behind us with stealthy persistence. He watches our every move waiting for a vantage point to steal, kill, and destroy. The gifts of joy, health, and provisions are grabbed away from us and our potentials destroyed even at the infant stage of development or fruition to stop God's good plan and purpose for us; individually or in groups. The ultimate scheme is to kill us, either with sudden surprise attack such as in accidents and natural calamities, or as a protracted struggle like a recurring or debilitating sickness. Accidents and diseases come to us, irrespective of our age or gender.

The author of abortion does not only abort babies, but also hopes, dreams, and aspirations that could have inspired the younger generation from the earliest time possible and those of young couples for their children. The increasing number of children and teens suffering from cancer, struggling with obesity and diabetes, or deluded into prostitution, as well as into gangs, drugs or any form of substance abuse, and all sorts of juvenile delinquencies are undeniable. Their health suffers and their lives are threatened with a dim future. With moral depravity perpetrated and commercialized by technology and media, marriage, home, and family are being shaken and shattered. The unending cycle goes on and on. Broken homes caused by irresponsible parenthood results in disillusioned children who are likely to become victims of myriad delinquencies and abuses to their own detriment and destruction.

Are these not images or shades of death in different areas of man's life? Many people think they are running from the shadows of death without realizing that they are living their lives with lifestyles that lead to walking, if not running, towards a living hell before physical death. This pursuit ultimately manifests itself upon their mortal bodies. The illusion, hypocrisy, and treachery of self-centered acceptance and acclamations, of fame and fortune, of position and possession, can engulf any person then destroy the life that should be lived with peace, joy, and fulfillment.

"The blessing of the Lord brings wealth, and He adds no trouble to it" (Prov. 10:22 NIV). The King James Version of the Bible uses the word sorrow for trouble.

The body that is temporary returns to dust. But the soul (the seat of the mind, will, and emotion) separates from the body and may face the judgment of greater damnation in eternal hell fires and separation from God forever.

> *"... man is destined to die once, and after that to face judgment,"* (Hebrews 9:27 NIV)

King David of Israel wrote Psalm 23 stating that though he would walk in the valley of the shadow of death, he wouldn't fear evil. Even if death is lurking behind us, we can still live life without fear. The howling intimidations of death have no power to destroy or shorten life. God is the author and giver of life. He is the sole authority and has full power to extinguish or extend life according to His will or purpose. The instigator of death is a thief who schemes to destroy or stop the life God gives. But the Shepherd of our souls came to give life and to rescue His sheep's life from impending death. Jesus, the Good Shepherd, declared the truth,

"The thief's purpose is to steal and kill and destroy. My purpose is to give life in all its fullness" (John 10:10 NLT).

The question is, "Are we the sheep of His pasture?" Jesus further declared,

"My sheep hears my voice, and I know them, and they follow me" (John 10:27 NASB)

The reason King David did not fear evil in the shadow of death is because of God's presence with him (Psalm 23:4b).

In one occasion when Jesus was teaching, some oppositionists threw stones at Him. Why did they do that? Obviously, they wanted to get rid of Him and kill Him. As always, He did not retaliate with anger or defiance. Quietly, He walked away from them. There were no arguments, no defenses, nor a word or sound. Was He being passive, trying to ignore them? Or was He just exhibiting His true nature by being forgiving.

We, too, can walk through life like Jesus, unaffected by offenses. We can address the negativities and uncertainties of life from the womb to the grave by truths, promises, guidance, directions, warnings, and assurances such as in the following Bible verses;

- Psalm 139:13-16 NIV, *"For you created my inmost being; you knit me together in my mother's womb. I praise you because I am fearfully and wonderfully made; your works are wonderful, I know that full well. My frame was not hidden from you when I was made in the secret place. When I was woven together in the depths of the earth, your eyes saw my unformed body. All the days ordained for me were written in your book before one of them came to be."*

These verses expose the truth that each person is carefully handcrafted by the Creator from the beginning of life that breathes, moves, and grows until completion and then is birthed out at His ordained specific day and time. Even the length of our days on earth, God knows and has appointed them before we came into being. His omniscience and foreknowledge include His benevolence for us to live with prosperity in all areas; He desires to bless us: physically with health; mentally with knowledge, wisdom, and understanding; emotionally with attitude and interpersonal relationship; financially and materially for sustenance in every way. His blessing and enablement affect our whole being to fulfill the purpose of God in our lives. In other words, God has a bright future in store for every newborn person. This truth will set us free from a defeatist self image, a low self esteem, a fearful anxious outlook towards life, and a myopic, warped perspective about the future.

- Psalm 119:9-11 NIV, *"How can a young man keep his way pure? By living according to your word. I seek you with all my heart; do not let me stray from your commands. I have hidden your word in my heart that I might not sin against you."*

This is a strong warning for the youth who are an easy prey to the wiles of the enemy of our soul. It also elucidates the precautionary measure for everyone to remain in God's word.

- Psalm 32:8 NLT, *"I will guide you along the best pathway for your life. I will advise you and watch over you."*

God grants a provision for guidance and direction as we travel along life's highways, byways, and subways amidst dangers, risks, obscurity or vagueness.

- Psalm 91:16 NIV, *"With long life will I satisfy him and show him my salvation."*

A promise for a long, satisfied, and fulfilled life. This promise is predicated by preceding troubles encountered in verses 3-8.

"For He will rescue you from every trap and protect you from the fatal plague. He will shield you with His wings. He will shelter you with His feathers. His faithful promises are your armor and protection. Do not be afraid of the terrors of the night, nor fear the dangers of the day, nor dread the plague that stalks in darkness, nor the disaster that strikes at midday. Though a thousand fall at your side, though ten thousand are dying around you,

these evils will not touch you. But you will see it with your eyes; you will see how the wicked are punished." (NLT)

Before, during, and after those verses are assurances of God's presence, enumerating His refuge, protective strength, and deliverance from the destroyer. However, God's deliverance is not something He automatically imparts upon us without our participation, but rather as part of His covenantal relationship with us. Psalm 91 begins by defining and delimiting who will rest in the shadow of the Almighty. They are those who dwell or live in His shelter. The Message Bible uses the words, "sit down in the High God's presence," which connotes a condition of surrender, of abandonment, of rest from self effort, and of contentment in God's reign, sovereignty, and control. We cease from standing up and lifting clenched fists demanding, insisting, and questioning. We cease from roaming around busy as a bee striving for what we want. Rather we sit down, resting from our own ways, and our exhausting labors. In God's Presence, there is fullness of peace and joy. This is akin to Psalm 23:1 NASB, "The Lord is my Shepherd, I shall not want." We simply let go and let God. He has all the armaments of heaven to shield us, rescue us, intervene on our behalf, and to fight and win for us.

Healing verses from NIV:

"for I am the Lord, who heals you." Exodus 15:26b

"Praise the Lord, O my soul, and forget not all His benefits – who forgives all your sins and heals all your diseases, who redeems your life from the pit and crowns you with love and compassion, who satisfies your desires with good things so that your youth is renewed like the eagle's." Psalm 103:2-5

"But He was pierced for our transgressions, He was crushed for our iniquities; the punishment that brought us peace was upon Him, and by His wounds we are healed." Isaiah 53:5

"He sent forth His word and healed them; He rescued them from the grave." Psalm 107:20

"Just then a woman who had been subject to bleeding for twelve years came up behind Him

and touched the edge of His cloak. She said to herself, 'If I only touch His cloak, I will be healed.' Jesus turned and saw her. 'Take heart, daughter,' He said, 'your faith has healed you.' And the woman was healed from that moment." Matthew 9:20-22

"When they had crossed over, they landed at Gennesaret. And when the men of that place recognized Jesus, they sent word to all the surrounding country. People brought all their sick to Him and begged Him to let the sick just touch the edge of His cloak, and all who touched Him were healed." Matthew 14:34-36

"Do not be wise in your own eyes; fear the Lord and shun evil. This will bring health to your body and nourishment to your bones." Proverbs 3:7-8

Sickness can begin right at the developmental stage in the womb with congenital diseases and then attack people of all ages, from birth to the grave. We are confronted with the lethal enemy of sickness and disease in our lifetime. We just don't know when it can hit us. We can face them either in agreement, confirmation, and resignation or with vigilance, prevention, wisdom, understanding, and faith.

"And the prayer offered in faith will make the sick person well; the Lord will raise him up. If he has sinned, he will be forgiven. Therefore confess your sins to each other and pray for each other so that you may be healed. The prayer of a righteous man is powerful and effective." James 5:15-16

During the Old Testament times, Hezekiah arose as one of the prominent and prosperous kings. He was a biblical example of God's miracle act of healing from a deadly disease. God extended his life fifteen more years. The scripture narrates in Isaiah 38:1-8 the following verses:

"In those days Hezekiah became sick and was at the point of death. And Isaiah the prophet the son of Amoz came to him and said to him, 'Thus says the Lord: Set your house in order, for you shall die, you shall not recover.' Then Hezekiah turned his face to the wall and prayed to the Lord, and said, 'Please, O Lord, remember, O Lord, how I have walked before

in faithfulness and with a whole heart, and have done what is good in your sight.' And Hezekiah wept bitterly. Then the word of the Lord came to Isaiah: 'Go and say to Hezekiah, Thus says the Lord, the God of David your father: I have heard your prayer; I have seen your tears. Behold, I will add fifteen years to your life. I will deliver you and this city out of the hand of the king of Assyria, and will defend this city.' 'This shall be the sign to you from the Lord, that the Lord will do this thing that He has promised: Behold, I will make the shadow cast by the declining sun on the dial of Ahaz turn back ten steps.' So the sun turned back on the dial the ten steps by which it had declined." (ESV)

No doubt that God heals all kinds of diseases including minor, major, serious, or terminal. This miracle healing that God demonstrated to Hezekiah was not merely for the sake of healing him. Surely, He is a compassionate God who heals. However, God transcends His loving kindness with a bigger, nobler, larger perspective and purpose for His actions. Instead of dying from sickness, King Hezekiah's life was extended fifteen more years, not only for his favor, but also for the sake of the kingdom of Judah. With his extended life, Hezekiah continued to rule with prosperity and success that other kingdoms became curious.

The almighty God has the power to heal and to deliver us from our enemy. He will not heal and extend our life for no reason and not merely for us to continue to exist, but to continue living a productive and fruitful life. Moreover, whether by choice or neglect, intentional or accidental, our life affects other people near or far. Our endeavors, may they be simple or complex, diverse or numerous affect others directly or indirectly. This is so because we are intricately interconnected with others. Therefore, God takes this matter into consideration. This is more pivotal and crucial in the life of a leader such as King Hezekiah. We may not be heads of state or country, but we are leaders in our homes as parents or older person, or as leaders in a group activity, in an organization, at school, or in some work environment.

When God heals us, He is also concerned about our family, our profession, our situation, and everything and everyone we come in contact with. This way we touch lives and significantly influence others for good to the glory of God. We are His hands and feet in His redemptive grace and transforming power in our world and as far as He leads us to reach. God's purpose and acts of healing and deliverance are comprehensive and expansive.

Let's Pray Together

*"I also tell you this:
If two of you agree down here on earth concerning
anything you ask, my Father in heaven
will do it for you."* NLT
Matthew 18:19

Gracious Lord,
Thank You for the life You extend to me each day. I acknowledge the truth that only You and nothing else, no one else, has the right, power, and authority to extend the life You give. Thank You for Your good and noble purpose of extending my life until this time and day. Cause me, help me, and empower me to live continuously according to Your purpose. Give me the courage and strength to tread on uncharted territories as You expand my borders; believing, trusting, and understanding that You are the prime mover of my life. Nothing happens by accident because You have ordered my path and You remove the rough road ahead of me. What then shall I fear? Nothing, except when I doubt You, when I disobey you. May Your gift of faith increase to higher heights as You enlarge my tent so I can be what You designed me to be, and be

able to accomplish Your designated assignment in the coming days for me, wherever or however you would want to expand or enlarge my life. This I pray for Your glory and honor, in Jesus' name, Amen.

Reflective Questions

1. What kind of extension have you encountered? Were they expected or not, requested or not?

   _____

   _____

   _____

   _____

2. How did you respond to an extension in any concern e.g. due dates of payments, deadlines of submission of paperwork in school or at work, or in any kind of extension? Do you consider it a favor or not? If not, why?

   _____

   _____

   _____

   _____

3. In what manner was there an expansion after you experienced extension?

   _____

   _____

   _____

4. How did your experience of extension in any manner affect your knowledge and relationship with God?

AFTERWORD

Death is Real

Death is such an obnoxious word most people ignore and evade discussing it. Why would I choose the word death as part of my book title? Death is real. To disregard its reality and the whole truth about it makes a person fake, plastic, and unreal. When we accept the truth on top of knowing it, the truth will set us free. As Ecclesiastes 7:2 (NLT) says,

"It is better to spend time at funerals than at festivals. For you are going to die, and you should think about it while there is still time."

In other words, accepting the truth of death is necessary, whether we like it or not.

Death begins to encroach on our doorstep from the moment of birth. In some cases, it commences the earliest in the womb. There and then, shadows of death start to appear, take shape, and tug along behind us waiting for a chance to devour us. To hide behind us is all it can do. It does not deserve an inch of our time and attention. We boldly face reality and prepare the best we can without fear and worry. Some forms of death are always with us.

- ❖ Famine, calamities, persecution, homelessness, bullying, hardship, troubles, tribulations, and dangers.
- ❖ Deaths of children, business closures, financial reversals, debilitating sickness, disloyalty or betrayal of friends, abandonment by spouses are incredible losses. Job knew such trials (see the Book of Job in the Bible).
- ❖ World War I, World War II, brought death as did plagues[1] as early as 430-427 BC in Greece with the Plague of Athens, the Antonine plague of 165-180 AD in Rome, the Bubonic Plague in Europe in the 18th century, the pandemic in China in 1855-1959, and the latest, "ebola," of the 21st century; the tsunamis[2] in Indonesia in 1883 and 2004, in Portugal in 1755, in Chile

of 1868 and several parts of Japan in 1498, 1586, 1707, 1771, 1896, 2011; and the super monstrous hurricanes[3] like typhoon Nancy in 1961 and the typhoon Haiyan/Yolanda in 2013 in the Philippines – the strongest recorded tropical typhoon ever to make landfall.

Death is not only losing your own physical life. One could grieve the loss of another person. My memory flies back to one Christmas day when my family was mourning the death of my younger brother. I was only seven years old then, but I still remember my father's bereavement from the time of his death in the hospital, at the funeral, and for months thereafter. I saw my father's hair unkempt, his face long, eyes misty, mouth shut from a smile or utterance. My little brother fulfilled my father's desire to have a son. At last, he came to our family, but my father's delight was short lived. I grieved too, because he was my only brother, an addition to my older sisters for my tribe of siblings. It was my saddest Christmas in the midst of a rejoicing world around us.

Or death could be the loss or end of something. One summer between my freshman and sophomore college days, our newly constructed house burned down. I can still vividly picture my older sister,

Concepcion, and I pushing a big cart packed with some of our belongings. I turned back thinking my father was behind us, only to see him standing still, staring at the house being devoured by the blazing fire, rapidly crushing the house from the roof to the upper level down to the lower level and ultimately to ashes. We were able to save only what our physical strength could handle. Most of our belongings were eaten up by the flames. For several months, my father had gathered choice wood and other construction materials for his house. He had saved sacrificially from the sweat of his brow. Witnessing the loss of his work all in an hour was devastating. With one look at his face, I sensed the frustration and grief gripping him. His countenance was forlorn and dumbfounded at the grim sight. The heaviness he was carrying must have slowed his footsteps away from the fiery furnace to find our place of refuge and sleep for the night.

Life is Triumphant

The good news is the blessed assurance that nothing – death or demons, today's fears or tomorrow's anxieties, can disconnect us from the love of God that is revealed in Jesus Christ (Romans 8:35, 38-39). We can overcome the horrors of impending death and

Afterword

rise up victorious champions because of His immense love. The Word that was made human and lived among people (John 1:14) did not only die on the cross to deliver us from sin, death, and hell. His powerful life over death will continue to act on our behalf by interceding at the throne room of God (Hebrews 7:25).

We fight the good fight of faith, and overcome, then touch lives with the strength, wisdom, understanding, and insights that flow out from those experiences. How can this life of faith and victory be realized without experiencing the hardship, misery, or scarcity that decimate you to nothingness; the anguish, sorrow, loss, terminal illness, or death of whoever that debilitate you? Each sorrow has its own kind of trial; each has its own triumph. Everything on earth is temporary. But joy comes in the morning. There is always a dawn after dark. There is a butterfly after the cocoon. There is the blooming flower after the bud. There is the gigantic tree after the tiny mustard seed. There is always hope as long as we live. We are nothing, but our Heavenly Father owns everything. We approach, we ask, we receive. He knows best; what, when, and how. We continue to trust that what is impossible for us is possible for God through Jesus Christ – the way, the truth, and the life.

After the loss of my brother, my father continued helping his relatives. He found a son, even sons, among his nephews and nieces. After the loss of our house, my father built a house in another town where we relocated. He did not succumb to despair, but fought the ravages and rose to live life. He would still find time to play his guitar and sing. I guess I inherited, not his musical talent, but his resilience.

So, we must give priority to enjoy our journey on earth, tasting and seeing that the Lord is good all the time, everywhere. Let us savor the sustenance of food, enjoy the provision for clothing and shelter; the benefits of family and friendships, the stewardship of finances and possessions, the peace of contentment and thankfulness. Let each moment give gratitude for God's benevolent provisions and entrust the rest to Him.

Life is Beautiful

Life is worth living. Look around – at the broad expanse of azure with huge cotton-like clouds – at the birds gliding and soaring up high – at the butterflies fluttering to flowers – at the flowers budding and blooming with varied shapes, colors, and scents. Look at the flowers – red anthurium, peach daffodils, blue hydrangeas, purple hyacinth, and baby pink gladiolus. Look at the trees spreading shade over the rest of the plant kingdom. Look at the grasses on the fields that wave in unison as the winds brush through them. Look at the pink flamingos and striped zebras in the zoo – the fishes in the aquarium, rivers, or seas creating sounds of their own.

Such sights, sounds, and voices that feed our senses and evoke an awareness of our beautiful world. God endowed our surroundings with beauty for our enjoyment. As an old saying goes, "Beauty is in the eye of the beholder."[4] Let us behold and appreciate the beauty. God created everything before He made man so that everything man needs is provided. He is not only concerned with our basic needs for survival but also for our aesthetic enjoyment and pleasure. Let us appreciate God's creation.

Life is a Choice

Life is worth living when right choices are made. We need to choose the iridescence that exudes the brilliance of the gem that we are in the sight of the Maker. At the same time we spontaneously, effortlessly touch other lives with encouragement and inspiration. Below is a comparative presentation of the contrast between the kingdom of light and the kingdom of darkness. It shows what comes from the enemy of our soul, Satan, and what he provides vis-à-vis what comes from God and what He provides. What they offer is reflective of what they are.

GOD'S KINGDOM OF LIGHT	SATAN'S KINGDOM OF DARKNESS
Life	Death
Love	Hate
Abundance	Scarcity
Peace	Confusion
Safety and Protection	Harm and Danger
Construction	Destruction
Health and Healing	Sickness and Disease
Unity	Division
Joy	Sadness
Friendship	Quarrel, Strife, Isolation
Acceptance	Rejection
Humility	Arrogance
Contentment	Covetousness, Envy
Forgiveness	Grudge and Bitterness
Courage	Fear
Strength	Weakness
Bravery	Cowardice
Encouragement	Discouragement
Wisdom	Foolishness
Inspiration	Depression
Growth and Development	Decline and Failure
Giving, Benevolence	Greed
Restoration	Annihilation, Stagnation
Mercy and Compassion	Hostility
Trust and Faithfulness	Betrayal and Treachery
Freedom	Bondage, Slavery
Truth	Lies, Deception

Afterword

The Bible is replete with examples and illustrations of each of these choices. The narratives and expositions show the consequences of each choice.

Without godly wisdom some choices lead to destruction (Prov. 14:12). Man is limited and so is his wisdom. On the other hand, avoidance of evil and any form of it safeguards oneself (Prov. 16:17). In the Old Testament, Moses was adamant in presenting God's offer of life or death. "Now choose life, so that you and your children may live and that you may love the Lord your God, listen to his voice, and hold fast to him. For the Lord is your life and he will give you many years in the land…" (Deuteronomy 30:19b-20 NIV). In the New Testament, Jesus Christ declared, "I tell you the truth, whoever hears my word and believes him who sent me has eternal life and will not be condemned, he has crossed from death to life" (John 5:24 NIV).

When despite right choices, circumstances come along our way that demand a response beyond our capacity to overcome, or to accomplish, or to reach, or to endure, or to persevere, or to bear, we can choose to carry our weapons of faith and hope. We are not made for misery in any shape or form, but enjoy the provisions of nature, using profitably the gifts and talents we are endowed with, not only for us, but for others.

After failure or mistake, we can choose to move on and give ourselves a second chance. After rejection, treachery, or broken relationship, we can choose to arm ourselves with love that is best expressed in forgiveness. Relish life–**living life**–dwelling restfully in the shadow of the Almighty that is higher than the shadow of death.

BONUS ARTICLE

The Travails and Triumphs of an Evangelist
By Rebecca D. Caigoy

At the 2005 Assemblies of God General Council event there were some brochures that attracted my attention. They were titled "Lost in America," "Reach America Coalition," and "Intercultural Ministries." I became aware of the reality that migrants in America are continually increasing, and Asians are the fastest growing group.¹

I belong to that group. Thoughts began to run through my mind, such as how many are Christians. I know they face many struggles. They want to achieve acculturation without jeopardizing their original cultural distinctiveness. They suffer agony for financial stability while working towards fulfillment of the American Dream. Then there is a list of interrelated concerns like family issues, loneliness, peer pressure, isolation, and a lot more. How many of them are hurting, sick, or even dying?

Whether or not they are believers, they all need Jesus. The Christian migrants are grasping for God's intimate reality in this challenging season of change. The non-Christian migrants are prospective victims of abuse and depression. Someone said, *"Man's extremity is God's opportunity."*[2] I asked myself, *how can I be part of God's work among them?* There arose in me a compassion and empathy towards such people for Christ.

At that time, I was serving as assistant pastor of an ethnic church. My focus then was serving God's people within the church as the senior pastor directed. All my energy and attention were centered on my pastoral duties, and my compassion for these migrants was relegated to the background.

Years passed. And then the time came when a burning passion for these migrants challenged me to launch out into the deeper depths of service, denouncing traditional boundaries of gender bias, of age limitation, and of conventional expectations. By faith, I began with nothing – no financial support, no team except my husband and my son, and no material resources. But my confidence was in God who made everything with nothing. I had His Word, and that is what these lost needed.

It has been about 4 years since my decision to accentuate evangelism in my ministry. Despite my beginning with nothing, the strength of Spirit-filled prayer, the Word, and referrals from Christian friends fueled my efforts to connect and witness. Eventually I started gathering some people with a mother-daughter special after a few months of connecting in various ways. The succeeding weekly meetings that focused on "Nothing's Too Hard for God" theme were short lived. The attendance dwindled to one, sometimes none at all.

Soon after two home Bible studies followed. After a third home Bible study began, a life-threatening coma struck my body. I was hospitalized for 10 days, six of which were spent in ICU with no assurance for survival. With meager strength after 3 months of recuperation, I managed to invite neighbors for a testimony about my ordeal. This led to another weekly Bible study. I finally fully recovered, and my other home Bible studies were resumed.

As the time progressed, I experienced diverse responses in my evangelistic outreach – rejection, excuses, religious bondage, desire for just social activity, gender bias, to willingness to know the Scripture, acceptance, hunger for more of God, etc. A family with the most number of household members remained faithful. They grew continually from almost no knowledge of the Bible to salvation, hunger for more of God, learning to pray, dedication of their children, and water baptism. Recently, these new believers are experiencing religious persecution, but the solid foundation of God's Word sown in their hearts has strengthened them against the raging attacks. They, too, have proven their commitment to the Lord Jesus and His Word, even in the midst of strong opposition from religious parents. My compassion grew for them for I walked the path they are treading now.

In all this, I learned seven valuable lessons in carrying out my evangelistic calling.

1. Obedience to His call will guarantee His abiding presence, even when challenged by obstacles and scarcity of resources (Matthew 28:20).
2. Trust in God more than people–including fellow Christians–is most important. People are susceptible to mistakes, so be cautious. Faith does not discount wisdom and practicality. Enthusiasm with lack of wisdom is risky (1 Thessalonians 2:4).

3. Let the love of Christ prevail in every situation. The passion for God and compassion for people, despite the storms, must remain untarnished (1 Corinthians 15:58).

4. Teaching the Scriptures to non-Bible reading and/or non-Bible obeying, religious churchgoers needs a lot of wisdom and creativity. The approach is different from teaching regular churchgoers. Adaptability and flexibility are always needed. Complete dependence on the Holy Spirit and submission to Him for the outcome is necessary. We simply do our part to speak the Word, and leave the rest to the Holy Spirit for conviction, repentance, and transformation (Acts 2:37-42).

5. Receptivity to the gospel varies for different people at different times. Patience and perseverance are antidotes to haste. Induced ripeness results in sour fruit (Ecclesiastes 3:1).

6. Cherish whatever is available to you–whatever time, resources, and fellow workers you have. Trust God for them to be useful and fruitful (Exodus 4:1-12).

7. Thicken your skin and brace yourself. We are sent as sheep among wolves. Be confident. We triumph

over our travails because the battle belongs to the Lord (Matthew 10:16).

ENDNOTE

[1] CBS News, Aug. 1, 2012; Notary Bulletin, Sept. 13, 2012; *LA Times*, June 19, 2012.

[2] "Man's Extremity is God's Opportunity"
John Flavel, *Man's Extremity is God's Opportunity, John Flavel Quotes*, http://www.brainyquote.com/quote/quotes/j/johnflavel/399277.html, (accessed April 16, 2015)

The above article was first published in Women in Ministry Mobilized E-Newsletter of the Assemblies of God.
Erratum: "hospitalized for 8 days", not "10 days."

ACKNOWLEDGMENTS

How can I give thanks to many people without giving thanks first to the One and Only One who inspired and guided me all the way from the start to finish? He was the One who prompted me to write, and then I followed by faith. After I recovered from coma experience before 2010 ended, I started writing this book. I simply followed to walk this unknown path of dream forgotten... of dream unfulfilled... and now a dream fulfilled. He was the One who comforted me when my first draft of four chapters was deleted. He was patient in healing my discouragement until one day He restored my desire to write. He opened the door for me to attend the Rewrite Conference with free registration. His vision, His provisions – Yeah! He was the One who bolstered my faith to recover the lost four chapters. He was the One who sharpened my mind to recall the experiences that march together like soldiers in the same cadence toward the same direction – the theme of this book. He was the One who took control of my life and made all things work together for good so that I can continue writing. He was the One who orchestrated His divine connections for editors when I didn't know whom I can approach. They are:

Cherie Walters – edited two chapters despite her busy schedules wearing multiple hats in ministry and was writing two books when I approached her.

Carlyle Castle – edited many chapters in the midst of hectic schedules as interim pastor. He was also busy with other activities in missionary outreaches, tutoring, and a part time job. Yet, he was willing to help a fellow minister. Thank you also for your prayers, Pastor Carlyle.

Barbara French – my teacher in Creative Writing class who edited and critiqued several chapters as well as the Introduction and Afterword portions. She's a gem I can't lose; I had to go back to her class after a long absence. I am honored and privileged to study under the tutelage of a connoisseur in writing whose experience in teaching "Creative Writing for Seniors" for 22 years is invaluable.

Acknowledgments

My classmates in the writing class whose comments furnished preliminary reviews in addition to their edits.

Anne Katz, my seatmate in the writing class whose edits stood out above the rest with her teacher-like critiques and edits.

He was the One who provided me with supportive ministers and pray-ers such as:

Pastors George and Shalini Pallil whose prayers, and support for God's servants in the LA Section AG churches are genuine and unquestionably recognized by their constituents. Thank you Pastor George for endorsing Pastor Carlyle to help me with editing.

Fellow ministers of LA Section SoCal Network AG who prayed for me during sectional monthly meetings.

Fil-Am pastors' wives of SoCal Network AG who immediately responded to my request for prayer for this book. Thank you Rose Lapasaran for your prompt action and for leading the prayer.

Fil-Am pastors at the November 2014 FELF meeting who prayed for this book. The meeting ended with prayer time led by Pastor Alan Dionson. Thank you Lord for the opportune time for this book to be prayed for by ministers.

Perla Mendoza, the quiet and unassuming first lady of Charisma Life Church for her prayer behind the scenes. The power of agreement was manifested as the two of us prayed fervently. I can't deny that prayer in the spirit jet-soaring to the highest heavens. Thank you sis Perla, you made me feel a motherly-love-in-action prayer.

Fellow women ministers of WiM (Women in Ministry) SoCal Network for your Facebook responses to my prayer request for this book.

My Bible study group and other people who prayed, are praying, and will be praying for this book that God's purpose be accomplished.

All your prayers cement my confidence that this book will touch many lives, build up their faith, strengthen their relationship with God, and even bring more souls for Christ.

He was the One who opened the door for Xulon Publishing to be my book publisher. My lavish thanks to Michelle Johnston who was more friendly than businesslike; to Jennifer Kasper and Elizabeth Marrero who responded to my queries as well as to Bethany Emerson and Jesse Kline for their marketing updates; and to other staff whose names I don't know but I'm sure were so gracious to keep up the brand of Xulon – "Serving Him by Serving You."

He was the One who guided me with a list of prospective endorsers. Thank you for this bunch of perfect choices:

Leland Ryken – his name sprang up first in the list. His commendations for my assignments in "Poetry and Proverbs: The Psalm and Wisdom Literature" confirmed my inclinations towards the literary. It's an honor to be a student of the author of several textbooks in Bible Literature. Sir Ryken had cleared the trail that I may find my fit.

Joyce Jones Moss – her quick and warm response is a delight beyond measure. Her friendship through the Aglow ministry transcends leadership titles and positions. Thank you Joyce for your endorsement.

Jaimie Bowman – how can I miss a writer friend, nice and kind, like her? Special thanks to Jaimie who was instrumental in my attendance at the Rewrite Conference. In the WiM facebook, she posted the announcement for need of volunteers at the said conference – the volunteers were guaranteed free registration. Aside from the information, guidance, and updates in the writing industry, I got fired up to continue writing this book. From then, the new friendship with Jaimie became a treasure to me. Her diligence to become an author (her book was not published yet then) touches other lives - and me. My extravagant "thank you" for endorsing this book.

Jim Gutel – his servant spirit has captivated many ethnic groups. Despite his current health issues and ministry tasks, his reply to my request for endorsement was quick and without qualm. I continue to learn from servant leaders like him. I am honored to be helped and prayed for by him and his wife Karla for my challenges in ministry. Huge thanks again, this time, for endorsing this book.

Barbara Gilliam – women pastors are rare and she is one of them. My applause to such rarity. Her stamina and cheerfulness are contagious enough to perk other women ministers to fulfill their destiny. Her fast response for endorsement lifted me up with hope, both as a woman minister and as a writer.

George and Shalini Pallil – pastor of pastors. I am blessed to be a recipient of their pastoral care. They knew I had been writing this book and they graciously included my prayer request during meetings of pastors. They extended their support by their ready reply for endorsement. How can I thank them less?

He was the One who provided a professional photographer in the person of Shannon Davolt. Her availability is commendable when the first photographer I approached couldn't make it. Thanks Shannon, you made me feel at ease in a photo shoot – my first ever.

He was the One who gifted me with a supportive husband, Leo, and son, Levi who were contented with any food in the kitchen when my writing took center stage rather than cooking. My son was patient enough to drive for me to buy supplies when I run out of printer's ink or paper. My husband's narration of the raging battle for life during my unconsciousness in the hospital, our crossover dilemma, and our car accidents were vital in writing this book. With an auditor's mentality and keen eye, he also read my manuscript and identified errors as well as the improvements – though not from a writer's point of view, but as a reader. It is said that those close to you are often taken for granted. I don't want to commit such an injustice. They deserve my wholehearted recognition.

He was the One who cheers me to keep going when I don't know how to move on to the succeeding chapters or when I don't know how to revise my texts according to comments from my writing class. I confess I could have not written and completed this book by myself. I owe everything to the One and Only Holy Spirit, the Helper, the Paraclete, who walks along side with me through life.

"Dear God, please bless all these people I am acknowledging now – the work of their hands and their efforts to be crowned with success – more abundantly. They are Your perfect provision for Your vision for this book. Amen."

BIBLE TRANSLATIONS

Scripture quotations marked NIV are taken from the Holy Bible, *New International Version,* Copyright @ 1973, 1978, 1984 by International Bible Society. Used by permission of Zondervan Publishing House. All rights reserved. The NIV Minister's Bible. Hendrickson Publishers, LLC.

Scripture quotations marked NLT are taken from the Holy Bible, New Living Translation, copyright @1996. Used by permission of Tyndale House Publishers, Inc., Wheaton, IL 60189. All rights reserved. Today's Parallel Bible. Copyright @2000 by The Zondervan Corporation.

Scripture quotations marked NASB are taken from the Holy Bible, New American Standard Bible, copyright @ 1960, 1962, 1963, 1968, 1971, 1972, 1973, 1975, 1977, 1995 by The Lockman Foundation. Used by permission. Today's Parallel

Bible. Copyright @2010 by The Zondervan Corporation. All rights reserved.

Scripture quotations marked ESV are taken from the Holy Bible, English Standard Version (ESV), copyright @ 2001 by Crossway Bibles, a publishing ministry of Good News Publishers. Used by permission. All rights reserved. The ESV Study Bible, English Standard Version (ESV) copyright @ 2008 by Crossway Bibles, a publishing ministry of Good News Publishers. All rights reserved.

Scripture quotations marked MSG are taken from The Message. Copyright @ 1993, 1994, 1995, 1996, 2000, 2001, 2002. Used by permission of NavPress Publishing Group. NASB/The Message Parallel Bible. Copyright@ 2004 by The Zondervan Corporation. All rights reserved.

Scripture quotations marked KJV are taken from King James Version of the Bible from Today's Parallel Bible. Copyright @2010 by The Zondervan Corporation. All rights reserved.

Scripture quotations marked NKJV are taken from the New King James Version. Copyright @ 1979, 1980, 1982 by Thomas Nelson, Inc. Used by permission. All rights reserved.

NOTES

Chapter 1
1. "Atenolol (Tenormin) is in a group of drugs called beta-blockers. Beta-blockers affect the heart and circulation (blood flow through arteries and veins). Atenolol is used to treat angina (chest pain) and hypertension (high blood pressure)."
Quoted in "Atenolol, What is Atenolol" [article online], available from http://www.drugs.com/atenolol.html, (accessed March 16, 2015).

Chapter 2
1. "Norvasc (amlodipine) belongs to a group of drugs called calcium channel blockers. Norvasc relaxes (widens) blood vessels and improves blood flow. Norvasc is used to treat high blood pressure (hypertension) or chest pain (angina) and other conditions caused by coronary artery disease."
Quoted in "Norvasc, What is Norvasc" [article online], available from http://www.drugs.com/norvasc.html, (accessed March 16, 2015).

Chapter 3
1. "Hamlet-like" – the word is used as an allusion to the soliloquy "To be or not to be" of Hamlet in Shakespeare's play entitled "Hamlet."
2. "Gaining Through Losing"
Evelyn Christenson, *Gaining Through Losing*, http://www.evelynchristensonministries.org/bookstore.html, (accessed April 17, 2015).
3. Nagesh Belludi, *Inspirational Quotations by Mark Twain* (#352) November 30, 2010 [article online]; http://www.rightattitudes.com/2010/. . . /inspirational-quotations-by-mark-twain/, (accessed March 19, 2015).
4. Jayson, *With Christ in my Vessel*, CYF Lyrics, (blog), August 11, 2010 (6:50 p.m.), http://cyflyrics.blogspot.com/2010/, (accessed April 17, 2015).
5. "Aglow began in 1967 with four women who expressed a desire to meet together as Christians without denominational boundaries. The first general meeting was held in Seattle, Washington, USA... Today, Aglow spans the globe! And it continues to reach out to women–and men–of every creed, color, and culture, and, through women especially, to families worldwide. Over 4,600 Aglow groups meet worldwide, about 68% of them are outside the U.S. (over 3,000 groups). More than 22,000 Aglow leaders worldwide minister in their communities and nations, to an estimated 17 million people each year. Today, indigenous leaders are overseeing Aglow groups in nearly 170 nations."

NOTES

Quoted in "History, About Us" [article online], available from http;//aglow.org, (accessed March 16, 2015).

6. Andrae Crouch, *Through it All*, @1971 Manna Music Inc., Hymnary.org, http://www.hymnary.org/text/i've_had_many_tears_and_sorrows, (accessed April 16, 2015)

Chapter 4

1. A rhema is a verse or portion of Scripture that the Holy Spirit brings to our attention with application to a current situation or need for direction.
   "In Greek, the word rhema means 'an utterance.' Therefore, the rhema word in Biblical terms refers to a portion of scripture that 'speaks' to a believer. In most cases, a rhema word received while reading the Bible applies to a current situation or need. In essence, the rhema word is timely and extremely valuable in a Christian's walk with God."
   Quoted in "What is the Rhema Word from God?" [article online] available from http://www.sharefaith.com, (accessed March 19, 2015).

2. "Only one life will soon be past"
   Quote: Only One Life, Twill Soon Be Past – Poem by C.T Studd, May 13, 2009, http://hockleys.org/2009/05/quote, (accessed April 16, 2015).

3. "Nothing's Too Hard for God"
   Nothing's Too Hard for God Media Campaign, http://www.nothingstoohardforgodcampaign.ag.org, (accessed April 29, 2015).

4. "It is well with my soul"

It is Well with My Soul, the Song and the Story, http://www.sharefaith.com, (accessed April 29, 2015).

Chapter 5
1. Cookie Holderbach, *Just a Little Touch Lord*, Old Time Bluegrass/Southern Gospel Lyrics (blog), September 27, 2014 (11:12 a.m.), http://cookie-holderbach.blogspot.com/.../just-little-touch-lord-from-you.html, (accessed April 17, 2015).

Chapter 6
1. "Hyponatremia is a condition that occurs when the level of sodium in your blood is abnormally low. Sodium is an electrolyte, and it helps regulate the amount of water that's in and around your cells." Quoted in "Hyponatremia Definition" [article online] available from http://www.mayoclinic.org; (accessed March 19, 2015).

"Hyponatremia refers to a low level of sodium in the blood; Hyponatremia may result from excess fluid in the body relative to a normal amount of sodium, or it may be due to a loss of sodium and body fluid; Symptoms are nonspecific and can include mental changes, headache, nausea and vomiting, tiredness, muscle spasms, and seizures; Severe hyponatremia can lead to coma and can be fatal; Treatment of hyponatremia involves intravenous fluid and electrolyte replacement, medications to manage the symptoms of hyponatremia, as well as any treatments for the underlying cause."

NOTES

"Hyponatremia refers to a lower-than-normal level of sodium in the blood. Sodium is essential for many body functions including the maintenance of fluid balance, regulation of blood pressure, and normal function of the nervous system. . . The normal blood sodium level is 135–145 milliEquivalents/liter (mEq/L), or in international units, 135–145 millimoles/liter (mmol/L).
Quoted in "Hyponatremia facts" and "What is Hyponatremia (low-blood sodium)?" with the article *Hyponatremia (Low-Blood Sodium)* [article online]; available from http://medicinenet.com, (accessed March 19, 2015).

Then
1. "what a mighty God I serve!"
What a Mighty God we Serve (African folk song), Hymnary.org, http://www.hymnary.org/text/What_a_mighty_god_we_serve_african, (accessed April 17, 2015).

Chapter 7
1. "Nissi" is one of the compound names of God – Jehovah Nissi. It means the Lord our Banner. Some scriptural references can be found in Exodus 17:12-13, 15; Psalm 60:4. Song of Solomon 2:4, 6:4; Isaiah 13:2, 59:10; 62:10.

Chapter 10
1. Related story can be found online at http://news.google.com/newspapers, Philippine Daily Inquirer; *Don Clowers Fire* at http://stevenwarran.blogspot.com; *Country's deadliest hotel Fire* at

http://www.iklimnet.com; *At Least 75 Dead in Hotel Fire* at http://abcnews.go.com, (accessed March 19, 2015).

Chapter 11
1. Map of Mindanao, Philippines [maps online] available from https://www.google.com, (accessed March 16, 2015).
2. Image of Toyota Tamaraw model, Philippines [image online] available from https://www.google.com, (accessed March 16, 2015).
3. Charles Haddon Spurgeon, "God's Hidden Ones" [sermon online, 1894 Sermon # 2367 p. 2, Spurgeon Gems and Other Treasures of God's Truth] available from www.spurgeongems.org, (accessed March 16, 2015).

Afterword
1. Plagues
   Jamie Frater, "Top 10 Worst Plagues in History," *LISTVERSE* [article online]; available from http://www.listverse.com, (accessed March 20, 2015).
2. Tsunamis
   Campbell Phillips, "The top 10 Most Destructive Tsunamis in History," *Australian Geographic* [article online]; available from http://www.australiangeographic.com, (accessed March 20, 2015).
3. Hurricanes
   "As Super Typhoon Yolanda (Haiyan) continues its destructive path across the central Philippines, it has already gained infamy as the strongest storm ever known to make landfall and the fourth

strongest storm ever recorded in the world. . . In terms of overall strength, Yolanda is officially the fourth strongest tropical cyclone in world history, according to Masters. He said that the all-time record is still held by Super Typhoon Nancy in 1961 at 215 mph (346 kph), followed by Super Typhoon Violet in the same year at 205 mph (323 kph), and Super Typhoon Ida in 1958 with 200 mph (322 kph)."

TJ Dimacali, "Super Typhoon Yolanda is the strongest storm ever to make landfall in recorded history," [article online]; available from http://www.gmanetwork.com, (accessed March 20, 2015).

4. "Beauty is in the eye of the beholder"

Gay Martin, *Meanings and Origin of the Expression: Beauty is in the Eye of the Beholder/* Phrasefinder, http://www.phrases.org.uk, (accessed April 16, 2015).

AN OPEN LETTER AND PRAYER FOR EVERY READER

Dear Reader,

When the Holy Spirit spoke to my heart with God's Word in Psalm 118:17, every word of the verse became alive. Foremost at that time was the confirmation of His instruction for my life. Secondly is the purpose of His instruction. The first was for me, but the second was for you–"I will not die, but I will live <u>to tell what the Lord has done</u>" Psalm 118:17 (NLT). You are a recipient of that proclamation through this book. I did not understand it right away when I received the message during the recuperation after coma; not until after I started writing. As I continued on, I realized that this book is to awaken or sharpen your spiritual sensibilities and build your faith in God, the Omnipotent, the Sovereign, the Defender and Protector of your life.

I believe that this book has touched your life in one way or another. I pray that God's touch on you will continue to move on… and spread to others… that many more will come to know Him in a personal and deeper way… and the glory of the Lord will fill each one's world… and all the earth .

Huge thanks for taking time to read this book. You can request for prayers or connect with me through the following;

- Follow me on Twitter/Rebecca DC
- Friend request or like on Facebook/LivingLife LivingPresence
- Email me at livinglife_2015@yahoo.com

Please do me a favor by writing a comment at Amazon for this book.

> Grateful,
> Rebecca

"Gracious God and Heavenly Father thank You for the access to Your throne of grace anytime, anywhere, and for whatever reason. Today, I lift up my dear reader to You for Your best blessing and most appropriate provision for his/her urgent need. May You crown his/her efforts with success in relationships, in finances, in

career, and in everything he/she touches. May his/her personal life be described with prosperity, health, and healing even as his/her soul prospers. I believe You are ever ready and willing to lavish Your people, Your children, with blessings because of Your extravagant love. No good thing will You withhold to those who trust You and wait on You patiently. So, please crush the works of the enemy that may hinder the way of Your blessings for this reader. Carve in him/her the character of Christ and develop in him/her the fruit of the Spirit so that all Your rich blessings will not be for self consumption only, but redound to Your honor and praise. In Jesus' name I pray, Amen.

LIFE VERSES

1980s
*"For the earth shall be filled
with the knowledge of the glory of the Lord,
As the waters cover the sea."*
Habakkuk 2:14 KJV

1990s
*"I am crucified with Christ: nevertheless I live;
Yet not I, but Christ liveth in me;
And the life which I now live in the flesh
I live by faith in the Son of God
Who loved me, and gave Himself for me."*
Galatians 2:20 KJV

2010s
*"I will not die but live
And will proclaim what the Lord has done."*
Psalm 118:17 NIV

ABOUT THE AUTHOR

The Lord Jesus Christ had transformed Rebecca from a self-righteous, religious advocate into becoming His avid follower and passionate servant. As God opened doors through the past 33+ years, she metamorphosed into a minister in different capacities: an intercessor, Bible teacher in Sunday School and women's groups, coordinator, organizer, leader, speaker in churches and body of Christ organizations, then preacher and pastor. Her writings too had changed perspective and purpose to align with God. Through radical faith in Him and His Word, she became a prayer warrior believing that victory is won on our knees – fighting for others, her family, and herself.

Rebecca's love and hunger for God's Word led her to biblical studies at Spiritual Renewal Bible Institute, at Asia Pacific Theological Seminary, and at Global University.

Against all obstacles, these experiences were enabled by the amazing ways of the Holy Spirit. Now, she fulfills her childhood dream – to be an author of books – for His purpose.

Aside from preaching in churches and speaking in women's groups, she serves as a Small Group leader at Covina Assembly. With her husband and youngest son, Rebecca has launched out into pioneering a ministry in Southern California.